Emotional Rescue

Prose, Poems,
Songs & Stories
To and From the Heart

By
Gary Edward Gedall
16/04/2019

Published by:

From Words to Worlds
Lausanne, Switzerland

www.fromwordstoworlds.com

ISBN: 2-940535-64-4

ISBN 13: 978-2-940535-64-4

About the Author

Gary Edward Gedall is a state registered psychologist, psychotherapist, trained in Ericksonian hypnosis and EMDR.

He has ordinary and master's degrees in Psychology from the Universities of Geneva and Lausanne and an Honours Degree in Management Sciences from Aston University in the UK.

He has lived as an associate member of the Findhorn Spiritual Community, has been a regular visitor to the Osho meditation centre in Puna, India. And as part of his continuing quest into alternative beliefs and healing practices, he completed the three-year practical training, given by the Foundation for Shamanic Studies in 2012.

He has now, (2014 – 2016), completed a DAS, (Diploma of Advanced Studies), as a therapist using horses.

His hobbies are; writing, western riding and spoiling his children.

He is currently living and working in Lausanne, Switzerland.

By the same Author

Adventures with the Master

REMEMBER

The Island of Serenity, Pt 1 Destruction
(Series – published or in preproduction)

Book1 :   **The Island of Survival**
Book 2:   **Sun & Rain**
Book 3:   **The Island of Pleasure (Pt.1)**
                'Italy'
Book 4:   **The Island of Pleasure (Pt 2)**
                'Japan'
Book 5:   **Rise & Fall**
Book 6:   **The Island of Esteem (Pt. 1)**
                'The Knights Tale'
Book 7:   **The Island of Esteem (Pt. 2)**
                'Le Morte d'Arthur'
Book 8   **The Faron Show**
Book 9:   **The Island of Love**

Non Fiction -   (published or in preproduction)

The Zen approach to Low Impact Training and Sports

The Zen approach to Modern Living
    Vol 1 Fundamentals, Family & Friends
    Vol 2. Work, Rest & Play
    Vol 3 Life Cycle

Picturing the Mind:
    Vol 1   **Basic Principals**
    Vol 2   **Fields within Fields**
    Vol 3   **Pathology, classical, traditional and
                     alternative healing methods**

Disclaimer:

**The characters and events related in my books are a
synthesis of all that I have seen and done, the people
that I have met and their stories. Hence, there are
events and people that have echoes with real people
and real events, however no character is taken purely
from any one person and is in no way intended to
depict any person, living or dead.**

Contents

Introduction

This work is the cumulation of almost 50 years of writing.

My writing career began during my years at Delamere Forest School, under the tutelage of Mr. Bernard Benjamin.

The first piece that I would call writing was an essay that went well beyond the demands of my teacher. It was a story of treasure hunters in Africa that ended up trapped on a small island and suffocated / eaten by an army of black ants.

Not a very jolly tale, but one that excited my creative juices.

The next major event, (as you will read below), was a class given by the most beautiful Molly Bell, during which she offered us the opportunity to experiment with poetry writing. Something that I continued from then and which I have never really stopped.

The other interesting event, while still at Delamere, when I must have been 13 or 14 years old was an afternoon when did nothing by note down everything that I heard people saying.

Little was I to realise that this exercise was to be the basis of my fascination with the way people think and express themselves.

The rest, as they say, is history.

Enjoy

Gary – Lausanne 16 04 2019

Walking

This was the second poem that I ever wrote, (the first was a cynical appreciation of the wonders of a hand-gun – 'The Wonderful Machine').

In or around 1970, (I must have been 12 or 13, at the time), our headmaster and my teacher Mr. Bernard Benjamin was called away for the day and was replaced by Ms Molly Bell.

She decided to give a lesson on poetry writing, (which was excellent, of course).

And rest, so they say, is history …

Walking

Hand in hand they walk
And the grass is green
And the roses, red
And the sky, blue.

Side by side they walk
And the grass is yellow
And the roses, mauve
And the sky, navy.

Far apart they walk
And the grass is brown
And the roses, black
And the sky, grey.

Alone, he walks
And the grass is gone
And the roses, dead
And the sky, black.

Introduction to the first two stories

Free 2 Luv is one of the stories that I wrote when on holiday in Italy, in, I believe, 2015.

It was the first of three experiments in style, using modern communication methods; e-mails, Facebook and SMS's, as a means to tell a story.

The second is titled Face2Face and is the second story in this anthology, but the third, using SMS's was less successful, so it remains unfinished.

What interested me here, was the challenge to create a cast of characters; that we never see, that might be known to, but never really described by most of the others, and yet begin to exist in mind of the reader as complete people, with stories, a past and relationships.

Of course, things are not always as they seem.

Free 2 Luv,

To : Mysecretlover@gmail.com
From : Therichbitch@gmail.com

Dear Secretlover,

It seems that my suspicions were right, and my bitch-from-hell mother is spying on us.

Jean-Luc was called in to speak to our family lawyer, Stuck Up & Snobs and they knew all about the family of Cecilia the Celeb.

S & S reminded him that either he marries a rich, blue-blood bitch or else his part of dad's estate will be iced for the next 10 yrs.

Sure he threw a FREAK but dad's will is controlled by this balding bigot and wouldn't listen to ANYTHING!! Good God the bitch is a PhD Assistant, it's not like she's selling underwear in Wooly's or something!

Keep you posted

XOXO

Therichbitch

****

To : Therichbitch@gmail.com
From : Mysecretlover@gmail.com

Dear Richbitch,

Don't forget to check that your browser clears its history
when you log out!

XOXO

Thesecretlover

****

To : Mysecretlover@gmail.com
From : Therichbitch@gmail.com

Dear Secretlover,

Just because I have beautiful, long, curly, sexy blonde hair
doesn't mean that I have a blonde head!!

Peeved!`

XOXO, (just the same)

Therichbitch

****

To: Carmen.desilvo@bt.uk.com
From: jenny.decastilio@bt.uk.com

Dear Carmen,

Any chance of coming over for a while this week-end, things are a little tense here in the big house and I could do with a little 'time-out'?

Say hi to Carlos for me.

Jenny

****

To: jenny.decastilio@bt.uk.com
From: Carmen.desilvo@bt.uk.com

Hi Jen,

Oldies away for the w-e, so come and hang out all you want.
Can you bring a 6 pack and some smokes?

Carlos says hi back.

C ya

Car

****

From: SolomonAndSchult@bt.uk.com
To: Adrianne.decastilio@bt.uk.com

Dear Madame,

As per your instructions, I am informing you be means of electronic mail of the latest developments apropos your children and your late husband's will.

As you are aware I have convoked your son Jean-Luc to visit me in my chambers this day, June 6th.

I had the unfortunate task to inform him that his current choice of partner and potential future spouse would not be considered as an appropriate alliance as stipulated under your husband's last will and testament.

Against his arguments as to the eligibility of the young lady, I had no choice but to point out, that not-with-standing any positive points in her personal favour; her origins, socially and culturally leave much to be desired.

Again he contested my point-of-view and finally I was obliged to point out that the social / economic standing of her family would leave the door open to financial abuses that I, as trustee and executor of his father's will, could not take the risk to caution.

I trust that this position continues to be consistent with your own.

I rest as always,

Your humble servant,

Steven Solomon Jr.

Solomon & Schult, Solicitors and Commissioners of Oaths.

****

From: Adrianne.decastilio@bt.uk.com
To: SolomonAndSchult@bt.uk.com

Dearest Old friend,

My position is of course still consistent with yours.

Our confidence is, as it always has been, well placed in your capable hands.

Please continue to keep me 'up-to-date' with any future developments.

With my kindest regards

Adrianne

****

From: SolomonAndSchult@bt.uk.com
To: Adrianne.decastilio@bt.uk.com

Dear Madame,

As you might or might not be aware, Master Jean-Luc has returned to our chambers this afternoon.

It seems that he has had the presence of mind to consult another solicitor to clarify his situation, if possible, more to his personal advantage.

He has criticised us for taking too long to respond to his request for the release of his father's money, reflecting that it has taken almost a year since his eighteenth birthday for our decision.

He then insisted that, even though I might have the power and authority to block his direct access to his funds, as a legal adult, he has a say as to where and how his money is invested.

As to his first remark, I could only apologise for the delay and from there, he could only accept my apology.

As to his insistence as to his right to 'have a say', in which institution or fund his money will reside, it seems that your husband's will, being silent on the matter, leaves the situation unclear.

I can certainly argue that I could not sanction any investments of an illegal, immoral or risky nature; however, it seems that I would not have the right to veto any reasonable request.

I leave the matter in your capable hands

And rest,

Your humble servant,

Steven Solomon Jr.

Solomon & Schult, Solicitors and Commissioners of Oaths.

****

From: Adrianne.decastilio@bt.uk.com
To: SolomonAndSchult@bt.uk.com

Dear Steven,

I am sure that Jean-Luc has not even he faintest intention to dabble in the world of finance, he is an academic and the son of a rich man.

He has never had the slightest interest in money, where it comes from, where it goes – it is all quite a mystery for him.

I am convinced that the advice that he has found has come from some university, legal student friend, who imagines that this 'threat' to manage his own investments might scare us into accepting this inadequate liaison.

I am not at all concerned about this turn of events so do not worry yourself either.

If there is any news from my side, I'll inform you immediately but until then, rest assured, all is in hand.

And one last thought, you managed to protract the proceedings after his eighteenth birthday for almost a year.

How long could it take you to investigate fully any company that he would wish to invest in?

With all my kindest regards

Adrianne

****

To : Mysecretlover@gmail.com
From : Therichbitch@gmail.com

Dear Secretlover,

It is time to launch 'plan – the perfect husband'.

Excited?

XOXO

Therichbitch

****

To : Therichbitch@gmail.com
From : Mysecretlover@gmail.com

Dear Richbitch,

No, I'm NOT excited, this is not my way of doing things.
I'd rather be open and straight and come out into the open
about us.

XOXO, always

The-I'd-rather-not-be-a-secretlover

****

To : Mysecretlover@gmail.com
From : Therichbitch@gmail.com

Dear Secretlover,

Our relationship can NOT be either open or straight; my bitch of a mother would never accept you, which is why we have to accept this subterfuge.

XOXO

Thetrickyrichbitch

****

To : Therichbitch@gmail.com
From : Mysecretlover@gmail.com

Dear Brainy, Tricky Richbitch,

I always thought that a subterfuge was an underwater boat thing ….

XOXO

TheStupidSecretLover

****

To : Mysecretlover@gmail.com
From : Therichbitch@gmail.com

Dear Secretlover,

If you were really that stupid, you could never have attracted me to you.

XOXO

TheRichBitch

****

To : Therichbitch@gmail.com
From : Mysecretlover@gmail.com

And I always thought that you only wanted me for my perfect body.

****

To : Mysecretlover@gmail.com
From : Therichbitch@gmail.com

And I always thought that you only wanted me for my perfect body.

****

To : Therichbitch@gmail.com
From : Mysecretlover@gmail.com

Not only but also ….

****

To : Mysecretlover@gmail.com
From : Therichbitch@gmail.com

And the same to you.

Sleep tight my love

XOXO

TheRichBitch

■■

To: Carmen.desilvo@bt.uk.com
From: jenny.decastilio@bt.uk.com

Dear Carmen,

Really enjoyed the w-e, sorry about the chair, did I really fall backwards off it?

You see, that's the danger of alcohol, you break things and you don't even remember doing it.

It seems that Jean-Luc is going to see the lawyers once a week now. Did I tell you that he went last week? Oh-my-God, now my memory's checking-out –

I'll have to ask my mum if she'll be okay to book me into a posh clinic full of drunken pop stars and film stars.

Don't bother to SMS this week, school's having a crackdown on phones and mum REFUSES to buy me another one if I get this 'Very Expensive' one confiscated.

So it's just e-mail, chat or just old fashioned telephoning.

Say hi to Carlos for me.

Jenny

∗∗∗

To: jenny.decastilio@bt.uk.com
From: Carmen.desilvo@bt.uk.com

Hi Jen,

Don't worry about the chair, you know that we don't have anything that doesn't come in a flat box with instructions badly translated from Chinese.

If you think that you must have been drunk on Sat., Carlos is still hung over ….

No, tell me about the Jean-Luc situ., I luv a bit o' gossip.

Carlos says hi back.

C ya

Car

****

From: SolomonAndSchult@bt.uk.com
To: Adrianne.decastilio@bt.uk.com

Dear Madame,

Thank you for the background information on Mr. Marcus Thurwood. My own sources also confirm that does indeed come from a distinguished family; good education, old money.

Madame Jennifer has requested that we begin the procedure to release her heritage, so as to coincide with her eighteenth birthday and the official engagement of the couple.

As I see no objection to this union, I am ready to advance in this procedure.

Please signal your approval.

Your faithful servant,

Steven Solomon Jr.

Solomon & Schult, Solicitors and Commissioners of Oaths.

****

From: Adrianne.decastilio@bt.uk.com
To: SolomonAndSchult@bt.uk.com

Dear Steven,

I am also of the opinion that this would be a good match but my 'man' has asked me to wait for some days before making a final decision.

I don't really know what he is expecting to find but I was also equally sceptical about him finding anything negative about Cecilia …

At the moment he is in her room doing something with her computer, she has a school visit to some sort of science research lab today, so I called him up as he asked me to, if any time she might leave it at home.

I will of course keep you fully informed if there are any
new developments.

Kindest regards

Adrianne

****

From: Adrianne.decastilio@bt.uk.com
To: SolomonAndSchult@bt.uk.com

Dear Steven,

It seems that 'he' has uncovered some sort of a plot. It
seems that Jennifer has been trying to TRICK US.

I know that it is hard to believe that someone as straight
foreword as her could imagine to do such a thing but it
seems to be the truth.

He promises to have some hard evidence by tomorrow, so
we'll just have to trust until then.

Until tomorrow

Regards

Adrianne

****

From: Adrianne.decastilio@bt.uk.com
To: SolomonAndSchult@bt.uk.com

Dear Steven,

It is true; she has tried to make fools out of both of us!
Marcus is a homosexual!

The whole relationship was just a rouse so that she could
get her hands on her inheritance!

No better than her dopey brother. I really don't know
where they get it from, surely not from my side of the
family.

And now the worst of it. It seems that she is secretly in a
relationship with an Afro-Portuguese man. His name is
Carlos de Silvo and he is the older brother of her supposed
best friend Carmen. It seems that he is always in their
house when she goes over to stay and seeing Carmen is
just a cover to see him!

If she comes again to see you, please feel free to confront
her with these facts.

Regards

Adrianne

****

From: SolomonAndSchult@bt.uk.com
To: Adrianne.decastilio@bt.uk.com

Dear Madame,

Jennifer did indeed come to my offices today and, as you instructed, I confronted her with your information.

At first she tried to deny that the relationship with Mr. Marcus was a fraud but after some moments she admitted it to be true.

I then addressed the issue of the young man, Carlos. This relationship she flatly denies.

I then asked her as to the point of the deception and her explanation was that she just wanted to have access to her fortune so as to be able to invest in a business project with Carmen.

I then informed her, that if she had a reasonable business proposition, she would not need to marry to have access to her funds.

However, the money, as paid up shares of a registered company, would be blocked from sale for the next ten years.

She took a moment to reflect on this and then, to my great embarrassment, ran up and hugged me.

After the story with Mr. Marcus I was, I am sorry to admit, not totally sure of her sincerity and your 'man' seemed very convinced about her relationship with this Carlos person.

So I took the liberty to pose the question of how we could be sure that after the money was transferred, she wouldn't go ahead and marry him after all.

We discussed various possibilities for some time, until one of us, I'm not totally sure which, came up with this interesting solution.

I was to keep my role as trustee and in the event that Jennifer should wish to live in a couple with a man that I would not be comfortable with, the control of her fortune would return to me until she reached her thirty-fifth year, (35).

I must admit that the formula sounds just and reasonable. Please take some time and send me your reflections.

Your humble servant

 Steven Solomon Jr.

Solomon & Schult, Solicitors and Commissioners of Oaths.

This e-mail is private and confidential and is only destined for the person or persons to whom it has been addressed.

****

From: SolomonAndSchult@bt.uk.com
To: Adrianne.decastilio@bt.uk.com

Dear Madame,

As of your last e-mail instructions, I drew up the contract as proposed.

Also as you have instructed, I have shown it to and asked the opinion of several other lawyers of my acquaintance.

There have been some slight rectifications but as the document is relatively simple and straight forward there has been little to discuss or to amend.

I called Jennifer and Carmen into my chambers this afternoon and presented the contract to them.

Jennifer asked Carmen to read it over with her but neither one had any criticism or comments to add so she signed the contract.

As trustee, having the power of attorney over your husbands' estate, I of course was the counter signature.

Two of my administrative staff acted as witnesses and the document became a legal instrument at two fifteen post meridian this afternoon.

As soon as the contract was signed and witnessed, I gave the irrevocable instructions to our commercial department to create a company in their two names and transfer the sum total of Jennifer's share of the estate into share capital, blocked from sale for the next ten years.

The girls seemed very pleased with the whole operation, they both hugged me and then they hugged each other.

They then kissed each other ON THE LIPS for a very, very long time.

Madame, I feel that maybe we have made a very terrible mistake.

Your humble servant,

 Steven Solomon Jr.

Solomon & Schult, Solicitors and Commissioners of Oaths.

****

Be Your Hero

We all go down from time to time. And last year, (2018), was a particularly tough year for me.

After eight years of working as a full-time psychologist, and being responsible for the administration of our group practice, and a six year battle to have our house renovated, keeping on eye on our two growing up children and accompanying my wife through a late pregnancy, I was often feeling pretty exhausted.

During one of these low periods, I realised that the strongest person that I knew who could help me face all these challenges was ….

…. Myself.

And so I set myself the task of writing an upbeat song to boost my energy and 'be a hero'.

Sometimes, the only difference between being and victim and being a hero, is your own state of mind.

Be Your Hero

When the world is feeling lonely
When the world is feeling glum
With no one here to take your hand
And nowhere else to run
You've fallen in a cavern
You know there's no way through
There's no else to call on
So think to call on you.

Be your hero
Be the one to save the day
Be your hero
Be the answer, when you pray
Be your hero
You're the winner, come what may
Be your hero
Be your hero
Be your hero.

When your road has led you falsely
Into a cul-de-sac
You cannot move on forwards
But there's no turning back
There is no passage round it
There is no gateway through
In this situation
There's just one thing to do …

Be your hero …

Blind, Matthew Murdock,
Perceptive, D. became
Modest, Diana Prince,
Proud Wonder Woman's name
Mild mannered Clark Kent,
A confident Superman
Lonely, Peter Parker,
Is really Spiderman
Gentle, caring Bruce Banner
The mighty green-skinned Hulk
Skinny Billy Batson
"Shazam" will give him bulk
Crippled Donald Blake,
Becomes immortal Thor
Just call upon your other self
You will need to do no more

Be your hero …

When the world is feeling lonely
When the world is feeling glum
With no one here to take your hand
And nowhere else to run
You've fallen in a cavern
You know there's no way through
There's no else to call on
So think to call on you.

Be your hero
Be the one to save the day
Be your hero
Be the answer, when you pray
Be your hero
You're the winner, come what may
Be your hero
Be your hero
Be your hero.

Face2Face

Friend request: 22:00

From Adam: Dear Duncan, I was given your name by a friend whose son was a pupil in your school last year, (not in any of your classes). He said that of all the teachers, you were known as the most honest and trustworthy. I am a newly installed teacher in the region, and I have a delicate situation that I would like to discuss with another teacher. I feel that you might have the experience and the integrity to help me. So, would you accept to 'be my friend'?

New Thread: 22:15

Duncan: Hi Adam, any way to help a fledgling colleague on his maiden flights. You can now consider me as your 'friend'. What sort of delicate situation? And why contact me through Facebook?

Adam: First, the second question. I am very uncomfortable with this story and even speaking directly to someone about it, is out of the question for the moment.

Also, if you feel that it could be helpful to share something of this with some other of your 'friends', they might have had similar experiences that could be of help to me. – I really feel that I am asking a lot, but I can't think of any other options for the moment – sorry.

My situation is this: I have a very beautiful student in one of my classes, who, I must admit, I could easily be attracted to, and she seems to be attracted to me. She seems to always find a pretext or other to be the last one to leave and to have something to ask of me.

Duncan: So is your question, 'do I go for it with her or not?'

Adam: It is that simple?

Old hand: Of course it's not!

Adam: Who are you? Duncan, is this message public?

Duncan: Bernard is an old a trusted friend of mine. I thought that you said that you would like me to share these posts with friends that I thought might be of help.

I have a private group of other professions that I share certain reflections with. Did I do something wrong?

Old hand: I am an ex-professor and ex head of department from St. Giles public school. I would appreciate a little more information from your quarter!

Adam: @Duncan. A bit of a shock, that's all, I didn't realise that you would share these exchanges without informing me first, but it is true, I did sort of ask you to do it. No, you didn't do anything wrong – just a little unexpected.   Bernard. I'm sorry if I sounded rude, I was a little shocked, that's all. As to more information about me, that I cannot help you with, I'm shook up so much by this story.

Old hand: And so I should think so, having any sort of extra curricula relationship with a student is TOTALLY against all rules.

Annie: Against all rules is it?

Old hand: TOTALLY.

Annie: Well, I for one am for going against the rules then.

Adam:	@Annie. Why are you so okay to break these rules?
Duncan:	Annie married the prof.
Adam:	Did you? How did it happen?
Annie:	Just as you would expect. Howard was my teacher; young, intelligent, handsome, just wonderful in every way.
Howard:	Could you just write that again; I might have missed a bit.
Annie:	Spying on me? Is there no privacy in this world?
Duncan:	@Annie. There are other people on line ….
Annie:	Sorry boys. So, what was a girl to do? I went for him; he really had no chance.
Adam:	No chance and no choice?
Howard:	There always is choice.
Adam:	But it must have been against the rules.
Annie:	We didn't care.

Howard: You didn't care. I almost lost my job
             because of it.

Adam: So what did you do?

Howard: I had a very good relationship with the
             dean. I went to see him and explained the
             whole thing. Annie got transferred into
             another section and I was warned to keep a
             very low profile until she left the
             establishment.

Adam: And after that?

Annie: We lived happily ever after.

Howard: As soon as she had left the halls of the
             school, as a consenting adult, there was
             nothing that the school could or chose to
             do.

Old hand: But you were both aware of the rules and
             acknowledged their existence and validity.

Howard: That we did.

Duncan: But that only worked because you had both
             decided that you wanted a long-term
             relationship.

Annie: That's right.

Duncan: Adam. I don't suppose that you are ready to commit to a long-term relationship with this student.

Adam: No, I don't think that is something that I'm ready to commit to.

Old hand: Then keep your hands off her!

Adam: Are there no other points of view?

Stevie: Hi guys, just logged on. Interesting discussion. Hi Adam, name's Stevie, also prof. Less rigid than some others. Work in a private school, rules not as sacrosanct. How old is this young harlot?

Adam: Seventeen, I guess.

Stevie: Legally, she has the right to consenting sex, just be sure she's sober when she does it. If she can prove that she was stoned or high, then you're screwed. Otherwise, it's just her choice to sleep with a prof.

William: It's a good thing that you're not a doctor or a psychologist; otherwise you'd surely have been struck off by now. There is such a thing as undue influence.

Stevie:	So speaks our resident psy!
William:	A teacher, with the power to give good or poor grades, has much influence over his students.
Duncan:	Especially if the student is pretty but not very bright.
Adam:	Sorry but I don't follow you.
Annie:	It could also be a form of sexual harassment.
Duncan:	@William. A teacher has much power over his students and it can influence the grades that he gives, however, if a student is attractive but not very successful, she can use her sexuality to try and improve her average. @Annie: Sexual harassment has become a dangerous weapon in the hands of not-so-weak, manipulating women. Either you give me what I want, or I'll denounce you for sexual harassment. @Adam. Is this young woman very attractive – how are her grades?
Adam:	Her grades are fine.
Old hand:	I still say better keep your hands off her.

Adam: Too late!

Duncan: !!!!

23:45

Adam: Things did advance more than I have told
            you. I think I'd like to give you some of the
            details, but I don't want to shock anyone.

Stevie: I surely won't be shocked and anyone that
            might, is free to log-off when-ever they
            might choose.

Duncan: @Adam. This is a space that you have
            asked to have, which I have opened for you.
            I have invited some of my friends to
            participate. @Stevie, (for once!) I totally
            agree with you, if anyone might not feel
            comfortable with what you wish to share,
            they are not obliged to continue.

Old hand: I for one will NOT continue, if you have
            done something unprofessional, I do not
            wish to know. Good evening one and all.

Annie: I for one will NOT be leaving, share all that
            you need to, maybe I can add some
            reflections from the 'other point of view'.

Howard:	And as someone who has succumbed to the wily charms of a student temptress, I feel that I can understand if you have erred from the academic straight and narrow.
Adam:	Now I understand why Facebook talks about becoming 'friends', in the space of only a few hours, I find myself understood and supported by people that I didn't know, as well as any friends that I've known all my life. For that I thank you all. ….

00:30

Adam:	This is not so easy to write and to admit but now with your support – I will.
	It was a late Thursday afternoon class, I must own that Eve, (not her real name), and I had been 'noticing' each other during the class – which is to say; she was looking at me – normal, I'm the teacher but I was aware of a softness in her regard and I tended to look more in her direction than in others. I found myself looking into her eyes, loosing myself there, just for the shortest moments before dragging myself back to my subject and the class.

It became a sort of game, an exciting, dangerous game, from time to time she would look away; write something in her notebook, hiding a floating half smile on her delicate cherry coloured lips. I was in a mad dream; teaching a class, talking non-stop, a general awareness of each and every student and yet, only we really existed, just the two of us in a classic courting ritual. A ritual that you can see most anywhere and everywhere; in a bar, a restaurant, in offices, shops, clubs the whole world over. And here we were, on a hot, lazy, Thursday afternoon, the last period of the day, most of the class already half experiencing a cold beer and a cigarette outside the local pub, just waiting for the liberating bell to announce the opening of these academic prison gates. But not us; no, relaxing, arm in arm, lounging on a bank of the softest heather, drifting on clouds of perfumed honeysuckle, gazing, no drowning in the eyes of the other ….

And yet the incessant droning of my own voice, like some deranged, insistent bumble bee, kept buzzing, on and on and on. The brain being such an incredible system;

I was aware of all these things; the class, their efforts to keep present, my interactions with Eve, her responses, my mechanical ability to continue to teach, while being totally distracted AND the ability to be in awe that all these processes that could function quasi-simultaneously.

I digress ….

Eventually the bell rung, and the class ended. I wasn't sure if I was relieved or frustrated that this extraordinary experience had come to an end. I was almost certain that she would wait for me, would find a pretext for us to be alone, if only for a second. The class started to melt out of the hot, stuffy class room, some, mostly boys, had tried for the world record of leaving the classroom as quickly as possible, others seemed to function in slow motion, as if the heat had sapped important life energy from their bodies. Eve was lost, digging deep into her desk, a friend stopped to ask her something – to go somewhere with her straight after school? My breath seemed to stop, she smiled, shook her head, 'no' and I my breathing normalised.

Centuries passed, the last student left, maybe it was just good education, maybe it was a type of intuition, but he closed the door after himself. I had just put my notes into my rucksack when I heard her approach my desk, I looked up.

'You've cut your hair,' she smiled; I could see that she was pleased that I had noticed. 'Do you like it, it's a bit short,' she replied, a little shyly. She had, had it cut quite short and it was quite curly. I wanted to touch it, to plough my fingers through it, to grab it, to pull her towards me with it. I knew that this was a moment of truth, a moment of choice, a decisional, maybe life changing moment. Touch her hair and open the gates of Hell or leave it be and risk losing Heaven.

Stevie: I hate to interfere in a delicate moment, but it's now been nearly 30 minutes waiting for your response, and now I really need to go to the loo but …. Good God, what happens next!

Annie: @Stevie. You really are the most insensitive of men. @Adam. If you feel the need to stop there, don't let any pressure from 'us' force you to go where you aren't ready to go.

Adam:	Thanks Annie but I really feel that I need to get all this off my chest. I hope that my literary style is not too boring for you, but it seems easier to write like that.
Duncan:	@Steve. You should be ashamed of yourself. @Adam. Please continue when and how you choose, I for one find your writing style very readable.
Stevie:	@Annie. I take umbrage to your assertion that I am an insensitive man; I am incredibly sensitive, only I care soooo much for what I am reading that I haste to participate in the denouement, so that I can support Adam in his predicament. Hence, @Duncan I have nothing to feel ashamed about. As for your writing style, Adam, we literary types just have to learn to cope with the lowbrow trash that most people accept as communication. I feel that the content and form of your narration deserves to be published.
Annie:	I was right, Stevie, you are a brute.
Duncan:	Guys, guys, can we focus please.

Stevie:	Focused.
Annie:	Please continue Adam.
Adam:	I could feel my hand wanting to move, to advance, to touch, to caress. Do it, don't do it? You know that she wants you to, you know that you really shouldn't.
Old hand:	But you are the Teacher – she is only the student!!
Stevie:	I thought that you had logged off.
Old hand:	I have felt a moral responsibility to continue to read.
William:	@Bernard. If you continue with this high moral tone, with the implied threat that you somehow might denounce Adam for what he has done, then it would be unlikely that he will be able to share any more of his experiences and he will find himself again excluded from any means of support.
Duncan:	Do you have a suggestion?

William:	I suggest that we each agree, formally, that what-ever Adam might choose to share with us, we will NOT attempt to find out his real identity nor inform any person outside of this group of what he has done. A sort of medical secret or professional secret agreement.
Annie:	Great idea, I agree.
Howard:	Me too, I'm in.
Stevie:	Does that mean no publishing deal? ….Sure I'm all for it.
Duncan:	@Bernard?
Old hand:	I have no interest in taking on a new career as a private detective, Adam's secrets are safe with me.
Duncan:	And with me too. Is that ok for you Adam?
Adam:	Thank you. Give me a moment and I'll continue.

Adam: My heart was beating, faster and faster, my
          breath, shorter and shorter. I knew that I
          was lost, even seconds before I started to
          move my hand. It was the look that passed
          between the two of us, a deep complicity,
          the release of tension. Weeks of building up
          the threat, the menace, the fear, the
          excitement, it was all there, and it was
          ready for that release. I know that I must
          take all the responsibility, as you have
          commented, I was the teacher, but it was
          also my physical action, it was my hand
          that moved, even if almost independent of
          my will. My hand twitched, turned, moved.
          My arm, attached to an invisible thread,
          pulled by a horned angel from somewhere
          heavenward, tugged further and further
          towards her face and hair. Yes, yes she was
          also co-responsible, not only did she do
          nothing to avoid or block the movement,
          her eyes and smile egged me on, supporting
          my advancing forward with a fierce,
          energetic charm.

          The contact with her hair linked the electric
          circuit between us; the lightning struck, and
          heaven and earth was finally joined.

The tension passed, positive and negative poles normalised, and we found ourselves unified. Her head buried into my chest; my arms tightly, maybe too tightly wrapped around her slight form. There was nothing to say nor to do, we were the world, the whole world. I cannot really say exactly how long we stood there but it seemed a lifetime. Was this love? Kindred spirits? Infatuation? Precursor before sex? All I could be sure of was that I didn't want it to stop nor did she show any signs of wanting to separate from me. I could feel her small chest pressing and releasing against my abdomen as she softly inhaled and exhaled, her warm breath gently tickled the hairs on my neck.

Yes we could stay like this for ever, except we couldn't. The school cleaners were bound to arrive at any time, and we couldn't allow ourselves to be found like this. I gently but firmly pulled myself away. She turned her head up towards my own, her eyes were blazing with excitement and passion. I was holding her at arm's length, fighting against her passion and my own, I wanted to take her, here now, in this classroom. To Hell with the cleaners or anyone else that might stumble in.

The danger just stimulated me more, I could see and feel that she was game, that she was ready, that she was mine.

Stevie: Why did you stop? It's been nearly 40 mins! Please, please, tell us what happens next.

Duncan: Perhaps that's enough for tonight, after all we do have jobs to go to tomorrow.

Adam: Sorry that I had to stop. I just needed to take a break. I would still like to continue a bit if you guys still have the energy and patience.

Stevie: I'm with you all the way.

Duncan: My morning classes are quite easy; I can get away with a shortish night.

Annie: I'm ok.

Howard: I have the morning free.

William: If I'm tired, I'll just offer some sessions of relaxation, it works in both directions.

Old hand: Anyway, I'm retired.

Adam:	Sorry for the anti-climax but I just gave her a kiss on the forehead, picked up my rucksack, turned and walked out of the classroom. Nothing to say in a situation like that.
Stevie:	Is that it!??!!
Annie:	Don't take any notice of him, I think that you acted in the only way possible.
Stevie:	That would be a woman's reaction.
Annie:	That would the reaction of a responsible adult.
Stevie:	Obviously that explains why it doesn't apply to me.
Adam:	Thank you Annie for your support but that doesn't solve my moral problems of what to do about Eve.
Annie:	I trust that the relationship has not ended there.
William:	Is there something in your own history that might explain your need for such a relationship?

Family history? Infidelity? A father daughter relationship that you're jealous of, with maybe your mother and her father or a sister and your father, maybe?

Adam: @Annie. No, the relationship has not stopped there. @William. Even if there was something in my history that might explain an openness, even a compulsion towards this type of relationship, it still doesn't help me deal with how to handle the one I'm in.

William: Understanding your own impulses might help you end the relationship and help protect you from repeating the same error.

Old hand: At last a bit of good sense. End it now and don't fall again.

Adam: If I end it now, it will surely hurt her feelings and then she might become vindictive. If she went to the school governors, I could lose my job and as it's only my first post, that could be disastrous for my career.

Annie: Quite right, you have to look to her feelings, not just to protect yourself but also out of consideration for her.

Howard:	Yes, both need to be protected as much as possible.
Adam:	You see the difficulty that I find myself in?
Duncan:	How is this affecting the way you treat her in the classroom?
Adam:	I have to say that it's bloody difficult. Sometimes I'm extra hard on her, as if I'm angry with her for what we've done. Other times I just want to take her in my arms in front of everyone and in those moments, she can do and say whatever she likes and it's okay.
Stevie:	And how do you grade her papers?
Adam:	She's not a bad student, so it's easy to give her top marks without exaggerating.
Duncan:	I would suggest that you try and give her slightly less than top marks.
Adam:	Why?
Duncan:	For 2 reasons; firstly, it is less obvious that you're having a relationship with her if you don't always give her top marks.

And secondly you will prove to yourself that her motivation is firstly to improve her grades, the pleasure and excitement of seducing the prof. only comes second.

Annie: @Duncan! How can you imagine to say such a thing? That type of thinking is more likely to come from Stevie.

Stevie: Oh no, my students, the ones that want to sleep with me to up their grades are often quite blatant about it. The one's that get off with the idea of bedding the prof, they don't give much of a damn about their grades.

Annie: Stevie, have you been drinking?

Stevie: Do you have any idea what time it is? Of course I've been drinking and, for your information, I still am.

William: Is there more that you have not yet shared with us that maybe we should know?

Adam: William, I'm sure that you must be quite a counsellor.

William: Sometimes one has to learn to read the silences.

Howard: I'm not following this at all.

Annie: I'm in the kitchen. Come down and I'll
            make us some tea.

Duncan: So there is more?

Adam: Unfortunately yes.

02:05

Adam: It was the next Friday, the week had been a
            sort of a mix of paradise and purgatory. I
            looked forward to each class that she would
            be in with excitement tempered with self-
            loathing. I had trouble sleeping, I couldn't
            eat, I wasn't interested in preparing for my
            classes, I was too ashamed to tell anyone of
            my situation, so I stopped communicating
            with friends and family.

Annie: In short, you were in love.

William: Not with the feelings of self-loathing and
            shame.

Annie: Righty.

Adam: Friday came around and the colleague that
            was to teach her class took off sick. I have a
            free period last thing Friday afternoon so I
            took it over for her.

She had planned a quiz and the synchronicity of her falling sick and my being available turned something in my head. I offered the class, if they could get more than 80% of the answers right, then I'd invite the whole class to my flat for a drink. It was of course totally insane, out of all the school rules but I had to get her to my place somehow.

Duncan: Had her behaviour changed at all in the week? Attitude? Clothes?

Adam: Yes, yes I have to say that she seemed to be making even more effort than usual. I think that she was wearing even more makeup than before. And I couldn't help but notice that her breasts seemed more, how can I put it? Present. She has quite small breasts, but they seemed to be more 'up and out'?

Annie: Girls often buy a bra just a fraction too small so as create that effect, although there are quite a few bras on the market that promise all sorts of uplift and enhancement.

Howard: Great to have a woman on the team!

Duncan: What happened next?

Stevie: Yes, please, what happened next?

02:25

Adam: I cheated the quiz so that the class finished with an 83% score – what the hell? We met some time after school in a local park and I led them to my flat. I'd already bought some drinks and prepared my flat for the invasion. My decision to only buy a small quantity of alcohol was not out of meanness but a strategy to keep them from staying too long. As soon as I would run out of drink, most of them would leave straight for the pub. I must say that my plans worked quite well, most of the class; almost all the boys and the majority of the girls left soon after the last cans had been emptied. There were a few stragglers, but I just asked them to leave after a while, I don't think that anyone noticed Eve had absented herself into the kitchen as the last few students grabbed their jackets and left.

02:55

Adam: I didn't go to get her, I just started tidying up. After some moments she entered and we continued clearing up together, there seemed to be nothing to say, so like Brer Fox's tar baby, we said nothing.

After the room was cleared, I hunted out a bottle of wine that I had secreted away and returned to feel shocked to see that she had lit up a cigarette.

'I'm sorry, don't you like people smoking in your flat? I saw the ashtray, so I thought that it must be alright.'

'Sure, sure it's okay. It's just that I've never seen you smoking before.'

'If it upsets you,' she moved to stub it out.

'No, no it's okay.'

'It's, it's just that I smoke sometimes when I'm a little nervous.'

'There's no need to be nervous.'

'Then why is your hand shaking?' I looked, and it was, my hand was shaking like a leaf. And that was it, we both started to laugh. We must have both been very, very tense, for the laughter was an explosion. We laughed and laughed, and we fell into each other's arms laughing and we held each other, and we laughed. Then we started to caress each other and we carried on laughing, I then pulled her into the bedroom and we collapsed onto the bed and we laughed. We threw off our tops, one of her nipples was peeking out over her little bra, I pulled the bra down to release it totally. So small, so dark and so very, very hard, I had to touch it, to kiss it, to caress it but we couldn't stop laughing.

It was like some mad adult, child's game,
there we were stripping off, our bodies
turned on, wet and hard, we were about to
enjoy carnal knowledge of the other and we
just couldn't stop laughing. I really don't
quite know how we managed it but we did
have sex; wild, torrid, unhindered,
unrestricted sex. It lasted hours and hours
until suddenly she jumped off the bed.
'What time is it?' the panic took my breath
away.
'It's about eleven.'
'Oh-my-God, my parents will kill me. They
don't know where I am'. She ran from the
bedroom only to return with her portable
phone in hand. She held it like it was about
to burn her hand off only she couldn't put it
down.
'Eleven calls in absence! Oh shit, Shit, shit,
shit.' She sat down on the edge of the bed,
my beautiful sex goddess and started to
howl. 'What the fuck am I to tell them? I
can't say that I've been here with you and I
can't ask anyone to cover for me, I can't
tell anyone about us.'
As if just by asking for it, a miracle
happened. The phone rang.
'Hi Judith, what's up? He dumped you?
The bastard. Where are you? No, no it's no
bother, I'm coming over straight away.

I'll phone my parents and tell them that I'm with you. Sure it'll be okay. Stay there, I'll catch a taxi and I'll be there in 10 minutes.' She turned to me, 'I'll need taxi money.' She then stopped; we slipped back into that silent joining, only for the merest moment. 'How was it for you?' I dared to ask. Again, she broke down into laughter, grabbing her clothes, she tiptoed over to me, kissed me on the forehead and snuck into the bathroom to get dressed. I offered her a twenty, but she insisted that £10 was enough and she left.

Stevie: Sorry to sound like an old record but would you say that she was drunk or not?

Adam: I don't think that she drank anything.

Stevie: Well, it's okay then.

Old hand: It certainly isn't.

Annie: No it certainly isn't 'okay'. What are your feelings for her?

Adam: Well I'm clearly infatuated by her.

Annie: But you're not in love with her?

Adam:	She's only 17, I don't know anything about her. She's only a student in one of my classes. I'm not even ready to settle down to a long-term relationship, so I doubt that she is.
Howard:	Do you think that she could be in love with you?
Adam:	We've never spoken.
William:	And exactly what is love anyway?
Duncan:	William. Maybe will can leave the philosophical questions for another day. It'll be getting light soon, so let's keep to the topic.

03:15

Adam:	Oh. I'm sorry, I've totally lost track of the time. Don't you guys need to go to bed or something?
Stevie:	We're all old enough and ugly enough to choose to go or to stay as we feel fit.
Duncan:	Stevie's right, we're all responsible for ourselves. Whoever stays, stays.

Annie: So what do you think to do about this
            situation?

Adam: Ask for help?

William: Always a good reflex.

03:30

Adam: @Howard. You slept with Annie but you
            were both in love and you stayed together
            and got married, so you don't count.
            @Stevie. You seem to be able to sleep with
            any of your students but somehow it seems
            to be okay for you and for them, so you
            don't count either. Does anyone know of
            any other profs that have had sex with their
            students that could give me some input?
            Please, I'm totally lost here.

Stevie: Well big boy, you're the expert on this
            topic, why don't you give him some of the
            fruit of your long experience?

Adam: Has another one of you slept with a
            student?

Stevie: Not just one eh?

Duncan: Shut up Stevie, you're drunk.

Stevie:	Not that drunk. What's the matter, a bit shy all of a sudden?
Adam:	@Duncan, is he talking about you? If he is and you've had any experience of this stuff, please, please help me. You are really someone who's advice I could trust.
Howard:	I think that we've all come too far this night to get nervous. Duncan, we all know and respect you, if you've slipped for a short skirt and a pair of long legs, I can totally understand, I've had my own temptations.
Annie:	You've never told me any of this.
Howard:	Put the kettle on sweety, I think maybe we also have stuff to talk about. I'll be down shortly.
William:	@Duncan, none of us are perfect. If I could tell you half the stories that I've heard over the years, they would make your ears curl and many of my clients are the most respected people that you can imagine.
Annie:	@Duncan, if you can think of anything that could help Adam to work through this tangled situation, I think that you should sacrifice a little your untarnished image to help someone in distress.

Old hand:	It could be seen as an act of charity.
Stevie:	Go on Duncan ol' boy, it'll do you good to get it off of your chest.
Adam:	Please Duncan, it would be so important to me.

04:10

Duncan:	Okay, if you all insist. I have slept with one or two of my students.
Stevie:	Per year.
Annie:	Stevie! Drunk or not, you cannot allow yourself the liberty to make jokes of this type.
Stevie:	Who said that it was a joke?
Duncan:	Stevie, you are one of my oldest friends, but you could easily become one of my oldest EX friends – capisci?
Adam:	@Duncan, I don't care how many students you've slept with, please just help me deal with this one.
Duncan:	Okay, just what do you want to know?

Adam: Did you love any of them?

Duncan: No.

Adam: Not ever, not one?

Duncan: No, I didn't love any of them.

Adam: Then why did you sleep with them?

Duncan: Entrapment, they sought me out.

Adam: They sought you out?

04:35

Duncan: What else would you call it? Short skirts,
             heavy makeup, tits hanging out of their
             tops. Looking at me with those big eyes, as
             if I was some sort of God figure. Feeding
             my ego, boosting my moral, filling all the
             lacks of my self-image. Of course, they
             knew that I would give in to their nasty
             manipulations, good God, I'm only human,
             just a man, flesh and blood.

Adam: So they manipulated you, each and every
             one of them?

Duncan: Each and every one of them.

Adam:	And you never led them on at all? Never offered to help them with some extra private tuition? Never suggested that being nice to you might go some way to improving their average? Never offered to take them out for a little drink to celebrate a good mark?
Duncan:	But they were all manipulating me, I had no choice but to go along with them.
Adam:	And you slept with them all?
Stevie:	No, he didn't score every time – did ya big boy?
Adam:	You've slept with a lot of your students over the years, haven't you Duncan?
Duncan:	I'm telling you, I was manipulated, I'm the victim here.
Adam:	So tell me Duncan, after these girls manipulated you, what stopped them going to the dean's office and getting you sacked?
Duncan:	They knew that they had manipulated me, and they also knew that if they tried to attack me, then the truth would come out.
Adam:	And what would that truth be Duncan?

Duncan:	That they had tried to influence me to give them good grades and if they would speak to anyone, then I would make damned sure that they would get thrown out of school and branded as a cheat who would sell her body just to pass her exams!
Adam:	And every year, one or two students force themselves on you in this way?
Duncan:	I'm telling you, it's not my fault, I can't be held responsible for the acts of these girls.
Old hand:	Oh, but you can! This is despicable; I cannot sanction what I have heard this night.
Duncan:	But we agreed that what was discussed here would stay between us, professional secret and all.

04:55

William:	What I wrote, which I will copy – paste for you was: 'I suggest that we each agree, formally, that what-ever Adam might choose to share with us, we will NOT attempt to find out his real identity nor inform any person outside of this group of what he has done. A sort of medical secret or professional secret agreement.'

It was to protect Adam that we all agreed, not anyone else. Sorry Duncan, you can't call us on that one.

Duncan: But can't you all see that I'm a victim here?

Annie: I'm sorry Duncan but I can't honestly support you here, I feel that you have been doing bad things for a long time now and it's time that you paid for your choices.

Howard: And it's the same for me too. I'm logging out, I'll be down in one minute.

William: As one that has the habit of holding heavy secrets, I do not feel that it is my place to denounce you but I would heavily suggest that you seek counselling ASAP. Good night all.

Stevie: I think that maybe it's time I got a little shut eye before work tomorrow. TTFN.

Old hand: I expect to see a copy of your resignation, effect immediately, delivered to my home by lunchtime tomorrow! Good night and good riddance.

05:15

Duncan: Adam, at least you should be able to
              understand my position.

Adam: Of course I can Duncan, I feel that I know
              you as well as myself.
              By the way, did you know that just by
              clicking on the button 'share', I can share
              this discussion with the 1,214 friends I've
              collected over the last 3 years.

Duncan: But why would you do that?

05:30

Adam: Because you didn't even remember our
              story. I hadn't changed any of it.

              You know, I should have tried to stick you
              for a 50, instead of accepting the measly 10
              quid for the taxi.

              I deserved better.

              Goodnight Duncan – Amanda.

Love Is Just A Four-Letter Word

This was a little poem that I wrote while, (I do believe), that I was living in London, around 1984 – 5.

I had somewhere seen an offer to enter for a poetry competition, the theme being something to do we love.

So, I sat myself down and wrote this ….

Love Is Just A Four-Letter Word

His clothes were chic but sober, hers were loud and cheap,
His bed was cold and empty, hers hot, but not for sleep.
Sex was always paid for, a minimum to survive,
Love; a four-letter word, money adds up to five.

He wanted something special, she was to stay 'til dawn,
'Dollars on the table', 'A cocktail dress be worn'.
He to wear a condom, she to call him Clive,
Love; a four-letter word, money adds up to five.

'Sex for cash' ain't easy, pride has little space,
So intimate a sharing, don't even know the face.
But once there is agreement, the moment must arrive
Love; a four-letter word, money adds up to five.

His flat was warm but empty, though for this dream he chose,
To make a special banquet, he'd even bought a rose.
To act as if she liked him, was what she must contrive,
Love; a four-letter word, money adds up to five.

And so to bed he took her, just held her 'til the dawn,
The morning saw her leaving, in silence she was gone.
Notes left on the table, she'd took the red alive,
Love; a four-letter word, money adds up to nothing.

Love you to death

This is one of my most recent works, written about a year ago.

For my 'day-job', as a practicing psychologist, one of the most difficult relationship problems that I need to explain to people is that of co-dependency.

Co-dependency comes from a relationship where one member of the couple has practical needs that they cannot assume; (problems due to dependencies; alcohol, drugs, etc., physical handicaps or other psycho-social fragilities).

The other member has some interpersonal issues that make long term relationships difficult, if not impossible to hold onto.

By linking to someone with important practical needs, (dependent), their partner, (co-dependent), is assured that they will stay in the relationship.

The co-dependent partner often 'enables' the dependent partner to keep or even worsen their situation.

However, the co-dependent member is generally very kind, generous and also often particularly guilt ridden if they feel that they are allowing their partner to suffer.

To explain this in a humorous, none threatening way, I thought to illustrate this through a story ...

Love you to death

The little creamy, white ambulance with its cheery, cherry red crosses sped daringly down the village high street, its sing-song siren warning pedestrians and vehicles alike, that it was on important business and that they should let it pass without obstruction.

At the hospital emergencies, preparations were already underway to receive the stricken patient. The orderlies had brought out the oversized, re-enforced trolley, barking and madly wagging their tails in excitement and anticipation.

Two inquisitive nurses, who were just about to start their duties, were debating about the new arrival.

"Oh, it must surely be one of the hippo ballerinas".

"No, I think not", replied the other, shaking her heavy head, her little bell tinkling in time to the movement, "I think that it is a circus elephant that has sprained her trunk."

It was at that very same moment that the ambulance arrived, and the answer to reveal itself.

The dogs sniffed and yelped as they pushed the heavy cart towards the back doors of the van.

The nurses, shy by nature, turned as best they could to catch sight of the new patient.

The back doors flew open but all that they could manage to see was an enormous mass of sugar plum pink taffeta being hauled with some difficulty out from the ambulance and onto the stretcher.

"Come Ethel, let's go to the emergency arrivals desk, and we'll be the first to know."

The girls could chew over any small bit of scandal for hours, but to be the first to find out a juicy bit of gossip, would give them status for quite some time to come.

They dropped onto all fours, for greater speed, and charged over to the admissions section.

"Well, dressed in pink like that, is it more likely to be a hippo or an elephant?"

"We'll see when we get there", she didn't want to be proven wrong, at least not until the last possible minute.

When they arrived, they were both shocked to notice, that the creature, what-ever it was, had the most beautiful cascade of blond flowing hair, on its head.

"Maybe it's a wig, artists often wear wigs."

But of course, it wasn't a wig, it was real, just as real as the beautiful, blue eyes and the cherry red lips of the young lady being interviewed by the admissions nurse.

"B-A-R-B-I-E."

"Family name?"

"Mrs Ken". The nurse had been working since the evening of the night before, her big round eyes were closing by themselves, fortunately she wore big dark glasses during the day, so it was hard to tell if she was awake or not.

"Mrs Ken?" she confirmed, suspiciously.

"Yes, I've been married to Ken for ages."

"I don't give a hoot, about your husbands' first name, what is your family name?" She shrieked in response.

Fortunately, at that very moment the doctor arrived, "it's okay Nurse Grey-Tail, we can finish the formalities at another time, I'll take it from here."

"Very good, Dr. Sly", she would be happy to let her colleagues deal with this one, she should have been back in her nest hours ago.

He gestured to the orderlies to push her into a consultation cabin, and then smoothly turned and followed them out, his bushy tale, twitching first left and then right, as he withdrew.

****

Ken rushed in, breathless and panicked, what had happened to his beautiful, fragile bride?

They allowed him into the small, white, sterile room, it would have been very difficult to keep him from her.

"Oh, Barbie, Barbie, Barbie, what has happened? I was so scared when I heard that they had taken you into hospital.

Please tell me that you will be alright, I couldn't bear it if something was to happen to you. You are everything to me, you are my day and night and sun and moon."

"Not to worry", he smiled, entering.

"Who are you?"

"I am Dr. Sly, and I am looking after your wife."

"He's very, very sweet," it was the first time that she had spoken, since he had burst in.

"Please tell me that you are going to be alright."

"Barbie is not in any immediate danger, although there are some very worrying signs that we have noticed after her basic examination."

"What do you mean? What worrying signs?"

"Please sit down, Mr. Emm?"

"Ken, my name is Ken, just Ken."

"Please sit-down Ken."

He tries to sit on the bed next to Barbie, but she is already overflowing the extra-size consultation bed, so he finally accepts to sit on a chair, which he has pulled up so that he can grasp hold of her hand.

"Your wife has a fracture in her ankle, not so surprising as she is morbidly obese."

"Morbidly obese, how dare you! I am always happy and cheerful, I will not, I can not be morbid, please tell him that, Ken."

"That's right, Barbie cannot be morbid, she has a sunny personality and is always full of the joys of life."

"I'm sorry if the term offends you," the doctor continued in a soft tone, "but it only means that she is dangerously fat."

"She has certainly never been dangerous. Barbie," he turned to her, "I do not like the way that this doctor is talking to you, I think that I should take you home."

"She is not capable to walk, and I would really, seriously suggest that you do not try to carry her yourself."

"And just what are you trying to imply about my wife?"

"Simply that she is much too heavy for you to lift."

"Maybe she has gained a few pounds these past few years, but she is in no way too heavy for me to lift, she is Barbie and I am Ken."

"Fine, I will ask for the release papers to be brought in. However, I still have an ethical duty to share with you the findings of our investigations."

"Fine, but please stop saying unpleasant things about my wife."

"I will simply inform you of the lab reports. Good. Linked to Barbie's 'slight' weight gain, she has a high potential of diabetes developing over the five to ten years.

Her levels of cholesterol are concerning, as is the strain on her heart, there are early signs of liver damage, her liver is under some stress."

"Why should her liver be 'under stress'?"

"There are of course several possible explanations, but the most common and likely is that of abuse of alcohol."

"Barbie would never abuse anyone or anything."

"I apologise," he wearily shakes his furry head, "I should have said, too much alcohol consumption."

"Alcohol? Barbie, do you drink alcohol?"

"But no, Ken, when would I drink alcohol, I never go out any more, and you buy everything for the house. You're so wonderful, you're my hero."

"And you are my angel, nothing is too much trouble for your comfort and well-being."

Ken stands, grabs Barbie's hands with his, coming closer and closer to her, then he stops, and the two lovers just rest there, lost in the depth of their love, lost in the eyes of the other, lost in the moment.

"Ahhumm," although the doctor's face and voice remain steady and calm, his tail is twitching in all directions, and his ears, as with angry horses, are pinned towards the back of his head.

The moment is broken and Ken, reluctantly releases one of Barbie's hands, so that he can return back again to his seat.

"The blood tests are conclusive; Barbie has been drinking alcohol regularly for at least several months."

"My wife does not drink alcohol, regularly or otherwise, is that clear?"

"I only have the results to go on."

"Then there has been some mistake."

"If you say so."

"Yes, I do."

"Ken, you are my hero."

"Barbie, you are my princess."

"There is just one other point."

"What now?"

"It seems that your wife is slightly asthmatic. It could just be a side effect of her weight or she might be sensitive to certain pollens. Do you ever suffer from hay fever?"

"Dr. Sly, I never suffer from anything, suffering is not something I accept, and as for hay fever, I never have fever, I am always in the pink of health."

"Fine, fine. I shall organize a bed for you."

"We will need a private room."

"Sir, this is a hospital, not a hotel."

"But I will be staying with her."

"That, I'm afraid would be totally out of the question."

Ken stood up quite aggressively and seemed like has was about to threaten the doctor when Barbie squeezed his hand.

"Ken, it will be alright."

"But we haven't slept apart for ever."

"It will be okay."

"I will not sleep until you are safe home again with me."

"Then you are likely to become rather tired, good night to both of you," and with a violent swish of his tail, he was off.

****

The next day the nurses were standing outside of Barbie's room talking amongst themselves.

"I just don't understand it at all, she refuses to eat hardly anything. A bit of meat, salad or vegetables, no sweet drinks nor deserts and yet she's as big as a house."

"She hasn't asked for anything alcoholic either, it just doesn't make sense."

It was at that precise moment that Ken arrived, he was carrying an enormous bouquet of flowers and a large rucksack hung heavily from one shoulder.

"Please could you find a vase for these, she likes flowers so much."

He handed the flowers to the nurse that had held out her hoof to collect them.

"Thank you," he said as turned towards the door of his most beloved.

Dr. Sly was also puzzled by Barbie's behaviour and how it conflicted with all the test results, so he had organised to be informed when Ken would make his appearance, so he could discuss it with them together.

He was much less confused after he had entered into the room, …. this is what he found.

Two large bottles of champagne, opened; one normal, one pink.

There was a large box of Turkish delight, half finished, a very big but empty box of cherry brandy chocolates and a well started monster box of milk chocolates, soft centres.

One of which, Ken, was in the process of placing into Barbie's open mouth.

"And just what do you think that you are doing?"

"These are visiting hours, and I am visiting my wife."

"And this?"

"This is an expression of the love that I have for her. I like to overwhelm her, to spoil her rotten."

"Well you certainly are succeeding to do that."

They both stopped what they were doing and looked at him, not understanding.

"You are doing more than spoiling her, you're killing her."

"But I love her."

"Okay, let us just say that you are killing her with kindness."

"How can he be killing me with kindness?"

"Barbie, you are obese, you can hardly walk."

"It doesn't matter, I do everything for her."

"… You are becoming diabetic, your heart is suffering, and as for the alcohol, isn't champagne alcohol?"

"No, not really, it's sweetness and bubbles."

"How often do you eat and drink like this?"

"Why every night of course, every night I stop off and buy her champagne, candies and flowers."

"Every night?"

"Of course, every night I feel so much love for her, I just have to show it."

"Isn't it romantic?" she lays back on the re-enforced bed, smiling happily."

****

"Please come in." Ken seems rather uncomfortable, the ruck sack is lighter, the champagne had been poured away and the rest of the chocolates distributed throughout the ward.

"Please, sit down," the fox is almost purring, Ken feels slightly more reassured, he had expected that the doctor was going to be aggressive with him and tell him off for having brought the champagne and candies into the hospital room.

"You love Barbie very much, don't you?"

"I don't think that I could live without her now."

"I don't doubt it," he smiles up at Ken, who is feeling more and more reassured by the doctor's tone and the way that the conversation was going.

"And I don't suppose that you can see any harm in the way that you are treating her,"

He starts to look confused; he shakes his head.

The doctor continues, "bringing her home chocolates and champagne every night, not letting her make any effort, supporting her not going out of house."

"But that is how I show that I love her."

"And yet it is doing her harm."

"So you say."

"So I say?"

"You, you're just like the others."

"What others?"

"The other people that are jealous, jealous of our love."

"Other … men are jealous of your relationship with Barbie?"

"Of course, they always have been, she's so beautiful."

"But now, she's not so beautiful, and she cannot even leave the house anymore."

"She is still beautiful to me, and she has no need to leave the house, I see that she gets all that she needs."

"Your house has become her prison, and you, her jailer."

"She's not in prison, she can leave any time that she wants."

"But she can't, can she?"

"I don't believe you."

"Why, because I want to steal your wife away from you?"

He stops for a moment, unsure of how to answer this wily adversary. He feels that he is being trapped, but he cannot work out what the doctor is after.

"Because what you're saying cannot be true."

"Why not?"

"Because I love her."

"Let me tell you a little story. Just relax for a moment and listen.

There once was a man who found a baby nightingale. He took it home and looked after it. He fed it with an old ink fountain pen, which he washed out for hours before using it.

Soon the bird grew; bigger and stronger, she was happy with the man, he was happy with her, he fed her and she sang for him.

One day he had to go away on a long journey, he could not leave this bird, the love of his life, so he grabbed her around the middle, with his hand, pinning her wings to the side of her delicate body and put his hand in his pocket to protect her.

She struggled for a moment, but finding no result from her efforts, she soon gave up the struggle and rested still in his hand.

Sometime later, he pulled the bird out from his pocket to feed her some seeds, but she was limp in his hand, she was dead.

The man was distraught, he had so loved this little bird and only wanted to keep her close. You know, we often kill the things we love the most."

Ken just sat, crumpled up on the chair, "Barbie is my nightingale, she is the most beautiful thing in the world for me."

"Then help her to be light enough and healthy enough to fly away."

"But if I stop buying her what she likes, how will she know that I love her?"

"By supporting her to find back her independence."

"But if she does not come back?"

"Then she isn't for you."

"How can I give her freedom and still be sure that she won't leave?"

"That, young man, you will have to work out for yourself.

****

Hello Dr. Sly."

"Hello, Ken. Did you succeed to work out how to give her freedom and yet reassure yourself that she won't leave you?"

Ken shrugged his shoulders, smiled at the good doctor before returning to the maternity ward.

Whispers in the Hurricane

This song was written on the island of Corfu on the 14th of August 2015 during the Deva Premal & Miten's Gayatri Festival.

Deva Premal & Miten are two of the most famous new-age singers and musicians on the planet, at this moment.

My wife, family and I had chosen to treat ourselves to a holiday of music, meditation, sun and swimming pool.

Which included participating in the festival.

But, why is the exact date so important?

The 14th of August is the birthday of Miten.

And in a talk or meditation, he mentioned the phrase, 'Whispers in the Hurricane'.

It captured my ear, and as it was his birthday, I decided to write a song for him.

He hasn't chosen to do anything with it, but I still like it, and thought to share it with you.

Whispers in the Hurricane

Words can cut,
Can bleed and stain
Words can bend
And twist your brain.
Words incite,
Aggress, inflame
Words can feed the hurricane

But
Words can bless
And words can love
Words can take
Us high above
Whisper loud
Whisper clear
Whisper softly
In my ear
Whisper Om,
Pure and plain
Whispers in the hurricane

Words can mock
And they complain
Drive you crazy,
Quite insane.
Drag your mood
Right down the drain
Words can feed the hurricane

But
Words can bless
And words can love ….

(Bridge.)

Whisper, whisper, to the one
Whisper
Whisper, whisper, never gone
Whisper
Whisper, whisper, to our love
Whisper
Whisper, whisper, shines above
Whisper, whisper

Words can bless
And words can love …

Words can sing,
 A glad refrain
Or dance a jig
Or plant a grain
They're golden sun
They're silver rain
Whispers in the hurricane

Words can bless
And words can love …

Words can sooth
 Releasing strain.
Words can cure
 And heal your pain.
Words can take you
 Home again,
Whispers in the hurricane

Words can bless
And words can love
Words can take
Us high above
Whisper loud
Whisper clear
Whisper softly
In my ear
Whisper Om,
Pure and plain
Whispers in the hurricane

Whispers in the hurricane
Mantras in the hurricane
Whispers in the hurricane
Praying in the hurricane

Whispers in the hurricane
Loving in the hurricane
Whispers in the hurricane
Whispers in the hurricane

My Funny Valentine

This was just I short story that I fancied writing a few years back as a sort of present to all my Facebook friends, (that now number over 4,500 persons).

As Valentine's day was coming up, I thought, 'why not write something light and romantic to mark the day.

Happy (Un)Valentine's Day to you.

My Funny Valentine

Yes, he certainly wasn't handsome, but then again, he didn't have a humped back and live in a bell tower either.

He was, however in love with the prettiest girl in the class.

"What are you doing?" asked his class partner.

"Ah nothing, Andy," he replied, embarrassed, covering up his project with his arm.

Andy, (nick named by their English teacher, after an obscure children's character, 'Andy Pandy', due to a similarity of ginger hair and freckles), wasn't going to give up quite so easily.

"Please, don't be mean."

"Look, if you must know, I'm trying to write a poem for someone, for St. Valentine's."

"I didn't know that you wrote poetry."

"Just 'cus I'm not good looking and all, doesn't mean that I don't have any feelings. Not like you, you got three cards last year."

"Yeh, but not from anyone I fancied."

"Well, I didn't get any, I never have."

"You know, even if you give one to someone, they won't know who it's from."

"I could write, will you be my Valentine?"

"And if they said no, then how would you feel?"

"Really bad, I suppose."

"But then again, now that you mention it, maybe it is worth the risk. You know, you could be really close to someone, and they wouldn't even guess how much they liked you."

****

"So, did you send it then?"

"No, I didn't dare, you're right, it's too risky, I would feel stupid and maybe people would find out and make fun of me. I'll just have to get used to never having a Valentine's card."

"So what's that on your desk then?"

"Oh shit, it's a card. I wonder who's it from."

"Why don't you open it up and find out?"

"Should I?"

"Don't be silly, please open it."

He slowly opens the card.

"Well?"

"Will you read it to me?"

"It's okay to close your eyes to wish, but sometimes you should open them to look, you might just already have what you are looking for.

Will you be my Valentine? Your best friend, Andy

(Andrea)."

Panties thro' the Post

This is a song that I really had to add, as it is linked to my own personal history.

It was 1979 and I was studying at Aston University, and still a virgin!

I met this very shapely, attractive young women, as the song describes, while I was 'on the door', collecting tickets for a student dance.

And she took me back to her room ….

And then, next morning, she opened a parcel sent from her mother, and in it was a pile of panties.

True story …

Panties thro' the Post

She's a very special lady
And she means so much to me
She took me in a baby
Then she set my spirit free
She always knew the kinds of things
That I needed the most
And her mother sends her panties thro' the post

I met her on a disco night
When I was on the door
She sure looked a pretty sight
While dancing on the floor
I nearly lost my job thro' her
For I was so engrossed
And her mother sends her panties thro' the post

She waited 'til the crowd had left
And took me by the hand
She smiled at me and kissed my lips
She knew I'd understand
I gained my spurs that very night
But something else I lost
And her mother sends her panties thro' the post.

I stayed with her all thro' the night
But when the morning came
She dressed and left without a word
Tho' I didn't know her name
Within the hour, she had returned
With a package from the coast
For her mother sends her panties thro' the post

When she was packing up her stuff
Her mum was sawing clothes
They then agreed to swap their tasks
For reasons, Heaven knows
But mother left the panties out
Concluded my fair host
So her mother sends her panties,
Her mother sends her panties,
Her mother sends her panties thro' the post.

Shame of a family

For a number of years my wife and I have been part of the FSS, (Foundation of Shamanic Studies), and have, over the years, participated many workshops and trainings.

Most of the workshops were led by the magnificent Ulla Straessle.

Somewhere around 2011, we shared in a Shamanism and Nature workshop, during which I was inspired to write several short stories.

Of these, two of them feature in this anthology; Shame of a Family and The Ugly Barren Fruit Tree.

I think that I must have been dealing with my own ghosts of being always odd, different, weird.

And, here, in that natural environment, somewhere, I was okay, somewhere, somehow, I was accepted and acceptable.

Shame of a family

Once there was a young man, not quite like many others.

He was quiet and nice, kind hearted and good natured.

He was healthy with a handsome face and beautiful, almond shaped, green eyes.

He was as educated as the next person with a fairly sharp mind and even, at times, a ready wit.

Unfortunately, his ready wit was rarely activated because for most of the time he passed his young life feeling rather sad and depressed.

And just way should he feel so sad and depressed?

Because the children in his village laughed at him, they mocked him, they made fun of him, they made up rude songs about him.

For, it is true, he was not like the others of the village, for one thing, he was much, much shorter than all the others and for another, he had very, very big hands.

So how come that this young man should end up so short and big handed? The answer lies as might be well expected, with his parents and grandparents.

The grandfather on is father's side was a Troll and the grandfather on his mother's side was a Pixie.

Both of his parents were so ashamed of their own parentage that they ran away from home at a young age and it was because of their shared guilty pasts' that they found themselves together, two half breeds, facing bravely a world where neither could fit in with pride.

Today was not much different than many of the days that preceded; the boys made fun of him openly, while the girls would cast him sly, mocking smiles and giggle together, all the time, half looking away.

What made today different, was that the one girl who had never mocked him or laughed at him or joined in a taunt him, the one girl that he allowed himself to dream of, to fantasise of, to hope against hope to be with, had destroyed his life!

She had announced that she had given her troth to another young man and not just any young man, the very one that had mocked him since the very first day that his mother had placed him with all the other young children in the village square on a feast day.

He fisted his huge hands in anger and frustration, oh how he would love to use these awful hands to beat and punch and hit that slimy, smiley oaf but of course he didn't, he couldn't, his hands were not for that.

His hands were for healing and soothing, often he would find an injured animal in the forest, draw it to him with the softness of a song and heal it with a gentle touch.

No, hitting the boy was not an option, fighting to win the hand is this sweet princess was not in his possibilities and anyway, even if she hadn't made fun of him, she surely would never, ever, ever think to give her troth to him.

As anger was not open to experience, sadness flooded in and then out through his reddened eyes.

Before he really knew what he had done, he had passed through his home, grabbed some food and belongings at random and ran away into the forest.

And so off he went, miles and miles and miles he trudged, night fell and he curled up in the protective roots of an old acorn tree and fell asleep.

****

He woke to the sound of sobbing; soft, simpering, sadness.

Cautiously he untangled himself from the roots and went to look for the distressed animal in pain and suffering.

At first he would he would have said it was a doe, huge, round brown eyes, fine, fine features, and the slenderest of bodies but with a long, blonde, flowing mane?

No, that just wasn't possible but of course not, for it was not an animal at all – it was a girl!

Maybe she was beautiful but it was impossible to tell; her hair was hiding most of her face, her body half hidden by the trees and the half covered in mud and dead leaves.

He moved gently towards her, a dead branch cracked beneath his feet. She turned her head towards him, her eyes growing wide with fear and panic.

"Go away, go away!" she cried out.

She hunted round with her hands and he saw that she had picked up something, maybe a rock or a cone, she was ready to throw it at him.

"Go away, go away!" she screamed again, her fear made her dangerous.

He stopped; he slowly raised his hands to show that he was carrying nothing in them and then took several steps backwards, before slowly sitting himself down.

He had seen this reaction before, and he knew instinctively exactly what to do.

He started to hum, very, very softly and then a little louder and then louder still.

Then he would add the words, the words from afar, words of a different language, words from a different world.

The words would sooth and caress the hearer, comfort and calm, they could tame any animal of any type, but this was the first time that he had tried them on another human being.

After a while she seemed quieter, he took to his feet and still softly singing he took a small step in her direction, smiling gently as he advanced.

She started, slightly but he stopped for a moment and she relaxed again.

Again, he started to advance, then stopped, then advanced and stopped and advanced and stopped and advanced and advanced and advanced.

Yes, one could now say that she was beautiful, the image of a frightened doe was still appropriate, but she was also a very beautiful young woman, in all ways that a young woman should be. –

Except for two small details, which at this moment lie hidden and secret.

"Are you not going to hurt me and send me away?" She was still scared, her great doe eyes, wide with fear and apprehension.

"Of course not", he smile at her, "why would I think to do that?"

"Because of these", she turned herself around and pointed to her legs and feet. On close examination he could see that her legs and feet were twisted inwards.

A strange feeling of joy washed over him, instead of feeling shocked or disgusted or even feeling sadness or pity for her, he felt, at last someone a little like himself.

Someone, almost normal but not quite, someone scorned and distained by all the others.

Someone who had suffered the pitiless taunting of the other children every day of her life.

Someone who couldn't cope with it anymore and had run away to try and escape a life of grief and loneliness.

Someone damaged and different enough to accept him as he is, small body, big hands and all.

His heart started to sing, his heart sang, his body sang and he sang.

He sang of loneliness and of rejection and of acceptance and of being accepted.

He sang of the trees, and the animals and the plants and the sky and the sun and the moon and the stars.

He sang of the seas and the oceans and the lakes and the rains.

He sang of sharing, of giving and getting and growing together and roots and branches and of linking and loving.

He sang with words and tones and sounds that neither he nor she knew or understood but surely, they did, for there they sat, linked with hands and eyes and hearts.

"Here, let me help you up", he took her small, delicate hands with his massive paws and gently pulled her up.

She took a moment to regain her feet, it must be a constant challenge to find and keep her balance with her legs so twisted.

On looking closely, one could realise that the problem started at the hips that must have been deformed somehow at or before birth.

The wave of energy took him by surprise, maybe it was due to his moment of rapture with her, but it was so strong that he shook with the force of it.

"May I?", it was asked as a question but they both felt that there was no question as to whether she would allow him to touch her hips.

Of course he didn't want to.

If he could do anything to heal her, even just a little, then she would be more normal and more acceptable and being so beautiful, surely some 'normal' young man would woo and win her.

No, there was no way that he could image to want to help heal her.

But he had no choice, he loved her, and we cannot allow those that we love to suffer if we can help it, even if it might mean losing them.

He placed his hands on her hips, his hands knew the exact locations, they began to heat up and to vibrate.

She looked at him, questioning him silently, he smiled back reassuringly, she relaxed a little.

He moved behind her, his massive hands sliding gently across her middle and back and then again fixed on the hips.

The hands slipped down to the tops of the thighs and they seemed to grow even bigger, they gripped hard, twisted and pulled back hard.

She screamed in pain, he held the legs in place, "no, stop, stop, please, please, please stop!", he wanted to, more than anything else he wanted to stop inflicting this awful pain on this fragile creature who he had begun so much to love but he held on because he loved her even more.

Minutes passed, they could have been hours of each of them.

It was if he was ripping her legs out of their very sockets, she screamed in shock and in pain and he cried for her pain and suffering but he held his grip

Slowly, slowly, slowly the pain began to subside, and the screams and the tears.

And then, suddenly it was all over, there they lie, both of them exhausted, exhausted from the efforts and the emotions and pain.

There they lie, gently holding each other, rocking, rocking silently to and fro, to and fro, to and fro.

Until, until, the movement stopped and together, interwoven, the two of them slept.

Some hours later, he awoke, it had become cooler, he was alone, as he knew he would be.

She had joined the world of the normal people and she would have no reason to stay with a man, a man with a shame of a family.

He was about to leave the spot when he heard a rustling in the forest.

He tensed himself, not knowing what type of person or creature he was likely to encounter in this place at this time.

It was a man, a man of about 40, 45 years, he was panting from his efforts, he was looking in all directions as he walked, he was looking for something or someone.

His eyes lighted on the young man.

"You, show me your hands", he demanded.

The young man, perplexed lifted up his hands.

"Okay, its got to be you or no-one, come with me".

He was confused and a little perplexed and scared, but he had the habit of doing as he was told, so he picked up his kit and followed the man through and out of the forest.

The man led him into a large wooden house; it was built on two levels, the home of someone quite well-off.

The inside of the house was organised as one might imagine, with a separate living room and kitchen.

He entered into a hallway and then into the living room which had several chairs and a settee placed facing a large, roaring fire.

There were two women in the room, a middle aged woman, who must have been very beautiful in her younger years, she was also quite small with pretty, fine features, she must have been the girl's mother.

So, if she was her mother, then the other woman must be …, he stared hard into a dark corner of the room where the other woman hid in the shadows.

"He's here," the man bellowed, as they entered.

"We can see that, you fool", answered the woman, clearly his wife.

She then turned and stared at the young man. "So you're the man that tamed and cured my daughter then?"

"Did it work, then?" His curiosity of the efficiency of the healing made him forget just how uncomfortable and scared he felt.

She came out of the shadows, smiling at him. "Look, I can walk normally; I think that maybe I could even dance."

A thought crossed his head, "what did you mean by 'tamed'?"

"Fortunately, you didn't know of her reputation before you chanced on her", smiled the father, "sit down, if you please, our daughter was teased as a young child".

"Maybe that is something that you could understand", interjected the mother.

"Yes, yes I do", he was starting to relax, he sat down at the end of the settee.

"Then you can understand that I had to learn to protect myself." It was the first time that she had spoken to him.

"Protect yourself?" That was something that he didn't quite understand.

"Oh she could be rather violent", her mother wasn't one to mince words, "but your singing seems to have as much magic in it as those hands of yours".

He was starting to feel uncomfortable again, "I think it's about time that I went, it's getting late and I've no-where yet to stay".

"What do you mean, no-where to stay? You'll be staying with us of course", the father was as direct as his wife.

"And", she continued, "we can't let the only man to have calmed our daughter and to have healed her escape like that."

"What are saying?" somewhere he was starting to panic.

"We think that you should marry her," the father smiled at the young man.

"But, but, but you don't understand. You don't know anything about me. I can't marry your daughter; I come from a family of shame".

"A family of shame", tears filled her doe like eyes, "what, what have they done that was so awful?"

"My mothers' father was a Pixie and my fathers' father was a Troll".

"And aren't we all blessed for that?"

"Sir, I don't understand".

"These young 'uns don't know anything", the mother continued, "where do you think those healing hands came from, your mother's, sister's cousin? They are Troll healers' hands. And the singing, that's Pixie magic."

"And those Pixie eyes ....", she was smiling straight at him, whole and healed, she still wanted him but why ever not?

He had nothing to be ashamed of, no nothing at all, he came from a proud heritage – pride of a family.

And so you Smile

And so you smile and laugh and song
Of honey bees in tender spring
Of baby's smiles, for love you bring.

So warm and soft, as tend'rest peach
Your body craves for mine to teach
And always just, so out of reach.

The Woman of my Dreams

In 2015 I thought to create a series of short stories to publish as 'Tasty Bites', this was one of them.

The idea came from a series of reflections on the theme of jealousy and fear of loss.

'What if you found yourself with your perfect partner?'

'What if you found that this person was not 100% - safe?'

'How far could you go to keep that person for yourself?'

'Is there a way through this?'

The Woman of my Dreams

As if in a Dream:

The sky was a very pale blue, an ultra-fine veil of cloud softened the hue and the edges of the tall buildings that rose and penetrated its lower layers.

I was walking in a type of forest; the trees were a sort of massive flower but without petals or blossoms, while at my feet, bonsai high trees flowered in abundance.

Butterflies as big as eagles soared above my head, humming melodies from the top ten hits of my youth, as I held a mature barn owl in the centre of the palm of my hand.

Of course, it was a dream but how was I to know I was in it?

Lost in the wonder and admiration of this incredible environment but if the place was itself extraordinary that was absolutely nothing when compared to the woman, who was standing, back against an enormous sunflower, smiling at me.

There she stood, faultless, the perfect height, shape, eye and hair colour, even her smile was exactly as it should be, in short, the woman of my dreams.

"Hello", it was a voice that I knew, from somewhere, deep, deep in my past, and the response came from deep, deep within my soul.

I felt the breath block in my throat, my heart beating hard and loud, I wanted to shout, to scream, to jump, to run to her, to grab hold of her perfect body.

Nothing happened, I just stood and stared, petrified like a frozen statue of myself.

She smiled; slowly, gently, warmly and the ice began to melt. I began to breathe again, to function, movement returned, and I succeeded to smile back.

Her gaze slipped down towards her hand, my eyes followed the movement, as in slow motion, her hand turned, and lifted towards me, inviting me to come towards her.

The distance between us was but a few metres, my desire to touch her was intense, but yet the time to arrive, into her waiting arms seemed eternal.

And yet; finally, immediately, there I was and here we were, flowing, melting, joining.

My body buzzed and burned and burrowed into hers. All my life I must have waited for this moment, a moment that would last forever....

"Today will be a good day".

"Shut up, leave me alone". I fought to keep her with me.

"Allow your body to deeply breathe in the mornings' energy".

"No! No, please, please, please don't do this". No, no, no she was slipping, slipping and fading away.

"Feel your body gently filling with the morning's energy".

'Damn, damn, damn', but it was too late, my morning, meditation alarm had begun its usual program.

She was gone and the dream, my most, most beautiful dream was already beginning to fade into the recesses of my memory and unconscious, The hard, real day had begun.

The Hard, Real Day:

It must be quite strange how the human psyche works.

One minute I'm all sad and angry that my perfect dream has been broken by my irritatingly positive meditation, alarm system.

And the next, here I am in the bathroom, immersed between my shaving and wondering how I'm going to hide from my direct boss that the work that just HAD to be finished by last night, lays, still unfinished on my desk.

I dress and am then further distracted by a bill that I have carefully left on the kitchen table because I really have to pay it, IMMEDIATELY, (so the reminder, gently informs me).

A bill which I have just found on the floor, several days later, hunting for the last clean teaspoon, that I have just dropped, fortunately, beside it.

I stir the sugar into my coffee, place the tea-spoon into the dishwasher, quite, quite full and congratulate myself for thinking to start it off.

The truth of the matter is, the choice to let the dishwasher fill up totally before starting it up is linked to my active 'ecological awareness', to run a cycle of the dishwasher, half empty is a terrible waste of our planet's limited resources.

Unfortunately, having disconnected any automatic reaction to start off the dishwasher, I then tend to have the problem to think to start it off at all.

The morning is bright and fairly warm, just as you would hope for a day in late spring; I am still taken by the bill that I must not forget to post and the concern about my boss and work.

The women are starting to show more and more of themselves as the spring progresses and the temperature and the hem lines begin to rise.

No more coats, more and more light jumpers and even some quite short dresses and skirts, sure to attract the attentions of unattached or poorly attached or even for some well attached males.

One particularly well-presented young woman catches my eye; I give her the north south scan.

Hair; thick, brown, well brushed, face; pretty, not too round or too long, makeup, noticeably present but not sluttish, nice body; well-rounded but not at all fat, clothes; well fitting, showing off well her figure, short dress, nice legs, high heeled shoes but not daft stilts.

– In short, the kind of woman that a man like myself could well fantasise to have an intimate moment with, BUT NO.

No, I'm not interested, not by her, not by the tall blonde with the large breasts walking towards me or the small, cute Asian girl with the Barbie figure and waist length black locks.

I stop in a moment of wonder, one might call it shock, there must be something drastically wrong with me, these girls are attractive, I should respond, my libido should notice and awaken, not be asleep in a lost corner of my psyche.

A letter box, yes, I remember, I am looking for a letter box. Well, here it is, I've found it but why was I looking for one in the first place?

Surely to post a letter, I have a letter to post, of course I have a letter to post, it's …. it's the bill!

Small problem, what have I done with it?

I search my pockets, feel the growing feeling of panic grip me as I come to realise that I must have left it at home, maybe still on the kitchen table, but yet. I really seem to remember taking it off the table….

My brief case, it was in the kitchen, it was open. With a now growing excitement I rip open the brief case and hunt through the various compartments, you beauty!

I hold up my prize find, feeling happiness and relief. Into the ever hungry, waiting mouth of the letter box I feed it in.

The bus is too full, I know for a fact that should I wait for the next one, which is very likely to arrive almost immediately after this one, (buses, like wild dogs almost always drive round in packs), it will be half empty, as everyone has crammed themselves into this one.

Why should this be?

Of course this bus has arrived twenty minutes later than it is supposed to, so we are all more or less late and 'sods' law informs us, (clause 18ii), 'if you are already late for an appointment and you wait for the next bus it will surely;

a) break down,

b) be driven by a driver on his first solo mission and get lost in the city's maze of one-way streets,

or

c) get high jacked by an ex-terrorist just dumped by his girl-friend

or

d) disappear into a black hole just twenty yards before arriving at your bus stop.

So we all cram inside like desperate Titanic party goers jumping into the last to launch life boat.

Happy to be aboard but wondering just the same, how on earth we are going to extricate ourselves to descend when we arrive at our designated stop.

(By the way, a small worry not experienced, so I have been informed, by the original, afore mentioned lifeboat patrons).

Have you ever wondered why buses have rails, high up in air?

Obviously to hold onto so not to fall over and into the rest of the passengers but not only- the rails and hand holds also serve another very important purpose.

It gives you somewhere for your hands to be, out of the way.

For having your arms by your sides, when the bus is jam packed full means that there is quite a high chance that sooner or later you will find your hand pressing against someone's body and both of you feeling quite embarrassed.

I was pushed against the back of a woman with wonderfully sweet-smelling hair, just a little shorter than me.

My right hand was safely attached above, and the briefcase was in my left, but I had to make great efforts not to rub myself against her every time the bus stopped or started, (quite often as one might imagine during the morning rush hour).

Someone was needing to pass from behind her to leave the bus.

True: there are now several games based on the idea how do you get a car out of a parking with the space full of other vehicles.

However; the bus departure dance game predates them by about half a century, but the premise is the more or less the same.

We all start to move in different directions, hoping to create enough space for the other passenger to create enough space for the person trying to leave to advance towards the exit.

As we all moved round, I took a half turn to the right, the woman in front, a half turn to the left, I took a half turn back to the left, while she took another half to the left and so there we were, face to face, nose to nose.

I looked, I gasped, I couldn't believe it, it was her, but it couldn't be, it wasn't possible but yet it was, it was really her …. The woman of my dreams.

"Hello", she smiled, amused at my reaction of shock.

"I, I, I'm sorry," I stammered, "I must seem ridiculous, staring at you like that". I do believe that I was staring and in a quite ridiculous way.

"It's alright, I'm quite used to it really", it's true, she didn't seem at all put out by my odd behaviour, she just kept on looking straight at me, smiling, "what's your name?"

"David, David Jones."

"Oh, how original". Feeling already slightly ill at ease, her reflection of the banality of my name was too much for me to cope with, so I did the only thing I could think to do in the circumstances.

"My stop", I blurted out and squeezed myself as quickly as possible out of the six wheeled, sardine tin and back into street.

Of course, I was still three stops away from my usual alighting point, but panic is a wonderful motivator for action and panicked, I was.

I could have waited for the next bus to come, logically, it couldn't have been far behind, but I had too much adrenalin pumping through my veins to rest in one place, so I carried on, on foot.

It just wasn't possible, it just couldn't be her but it really was.

Or maybe it was just my mind playing a trick.

The vague image from the fading memory of my dream hooking itself onto a generally, similar looking woman.

And yet, why should a woman, and a very beautiful woman at that, start a conversation with me, smile at me, ask me my name?

It didn't make any sense to me.

I was still so taken with my reflections about her that I had totally zapped the fact I was hoping to avoid my boss, having not finished my work for him, last night.

And now, there he was, entering the building at the same as I arrived.

"Morning, Bob," I smiled, "good night last night?"

"Not bad Dave, not bad at all." We drifted into the office and flowed over to our respective work spaces.

Work is a weird thing. In one moment, it can seem to be an insurmountable mountain complicated and confused, you turn your head and its fine; clear and straight forward; one, two, three and hop, it's done.

"Dave", the intercom sings my name, "did you finish that dossier from last night?" the question was light, without much tension in the voice but just the same, my boss wants to know if his work was finished when it should have been.

"Sorry, no Bob", I find myself answering, my honestly must surprise him as much as it surprised me.

"What was that Dave?" Yep, just as surprised as I was, now I am just as intrigued to hear my response as he must be.

"Yes, I was really, really tired last night, so I thought to take off just after you, buy myself a kebab and watch a film before turning in. It did me a lot of good."

"And what about my dossier?" his tone of voice has lost that careful neutrality that he had spent months and months perfecting last year with his private career coach.

"Well it's done of course; you did say that it was important. After relaxing last night, I was so on form this morning that I polished it off in next to no time. Should I bring it up now?"

The silence was really golden, never, in all the years that I had worked for Bob had he been lost for words but now, this morning, I had scored a victory unparalleled in the history of the firm.

"No, no, it's okay, I'm coming down later, I'll pick it up then."

"Right o", I responded gaily, "when-ever you want", and flicked off the intercom with the casual movement of Captain Kirk at the end of another successful mission.

'And you meet, but not merely by chance':

The rest of the day passed incredibly calmly, Bob was particularly reasonable with his demands and the rest of the team all seamed unusually friendly and available and most surprisingly I was able to focus on my work much more than usual.

Five o'clock, or to be totally accurate in our digital age, seventeen, zero, zero, suddenly appeared on the face of the clock on my desk.

Bob had not appeared all day so that 'very important' dossier still lay relaxing on a corner of my desk.

I reflected on the competing merits of taking it up to his office on my way out but after some little thought, the sense of victory to present it to him, face to face would more than likely cost me dearly tomorrow, so I let it drop.

I was quite immersed in the important reflection as to whether I would buy a take-away tonight on the way home or bung something into the microwave when I got onto my usual bus.

I have long since stopped to marvel how buses are always on time when we are in absolutely no hurry what-so-ever but surely it is just part of some complex universal law.

I sat down on an empty seat, not remarking that to have a double seat free for myself was in itself unusual and just the same it didn't stay empty for long.

I have taken the habit since being quite young, when-ever I would have the chance to sit on the window side of a seat to look fixedly out of the window.

This would avoid any possibility of noticing or being noticed by anyone that I didn't much want to be in contact with – most of everybody.

"Hello David", I jumped, had I fallen asleep there in the bus? Was I again dreaming of her?

"Are you asleep?", I don't know, maybe I am. I turned to look at my neighbour and there she was again, smiling openly at me, warmth and friendliness radiating from her sweet face.

"You haven't forgotten me, have you?" she was laughing at me, we both knew that I wasn't capable to forget her.

"Hello again," I think that I might have blushed, in any case I felt really hot and flustered, I stopped there, I couldn't think of anything else to say.

She continued looking at me, enjoying my discomfort in a lightly amused way.

"Is this your regular bus then?" I finally blurted out.

"No, I must have been drawn to take it to meet you, David". I still couldn't work out if she was being serious or not.

"This is my stop, I have to get off here", this time it really was.

"Would you like me to get off with you?"

"Yes, yes that would be really nice but aren't you going home or somewhere?"

"If you would like me to come with you, I would be very willing to come."

"Please, please, please come, we could stop for dinner somewhere."

"That would be very nice." We got off the bus at Ronald's Wood and then turned down Queen's Road where there is a very nice and not too expensive Chinese restaurant.

"Do you eat Chinese?"

"Do I eat Chinese, what?"

"Chinese food, do you like Chinese food?"

"I would love to share some Chinese food with you David".

There was something really strange about the way that she used my name. She stopped, ever so slightly, before very clearly enunciating it, as if to savour the moment.

Now I have had relationships in the past and the women that I was with all, pretty much, were in love with me at the beginning, (things didn't always pan-out so well, actually never), but this was different.

Firstly, in all the other relationships there was a clear moment of meeting, we would look at each other; across a table, across a bar-room, once, even across a photocopier.

But on each occasion, there was a moment when we both sent out and received a signal of mutual interest and from there on the relationship started.

Once it took us all of two weeks before we exchanged our first words but we both already knew that something was likely to happen – the agreement already existed.

Now she, she was surely in love me; in love with my face, with my eyes, even with my name but other than in my dream, I had absolutely no memory of ever having seen her before.

Yes, of course it is possible that I had noticed her, maybe on the bus, out of the corner of my eye, unconsciously and had then dreamt of her.

Yes, but that still cannot explain how or why she could be so in love with me.

The meal was all I could have dreamt that a romantic first meal would be; she was eager to try anything that I proposed, which we shared together, both eating with pleasure and relish.

She asked me question after question about my life and family, listening attentively to all the details, laughing sweetly at my little jokes, being concerned about my problems and supportive of my mishaps.

A Waking Dream:

It was getting chilly as we left the warm, scented restaurant, "shall I walk you home?"

"Wouldn't you prefer that I come home with you?"

I stopped breathing, I played back her response in my head, I looked closely to see if there were any signs that she was playing with me.

"You would like to come home with me?"

"Oh, don't you want me to?" she seemed genuinely shocked, hurt and surprised.

"Oh yes, yes I do but, but, but my place is a bit of a mess".

"Not to worry, we can tidy it."

"It's actually very messy," I had remembered clearly the state in which I had left it in.

"You really don't want me to come then?"

"It's messy, it's very messy".

I was starting to panic, if I invited her back and she sore the sight of my apartment then she would know the sort of slob that I am and would never return.

Yet I could see that by saying no, she was getting upset and might well take it as type of rejection and some women take rejection very badly and then, for that I might never see her again.

Genius!

"Why don't we go to your place?" suddenly it was her turn to look uncomfortable.

"I'm sorry David but that is just not possible, we'll just have to go to your place and tidy it up together. Don't worry about the mess; I'm sure that I've seen worse".

So I shrugged my shoulders and led her to my disaster of a flat.

… And she took it well, hardly batting an eyelash she took off her coat, kicked off her heels and set to work.

In a little more than half an hour the place was quite presentable

The neighbours would have been rather surprised to hear someone hoovering at that hour of the night as the person that comes in to clean and tidy for me, comes on Tuesday and Friday afternoons, (I admit to being a little ashamed to say it but it's my mother).

"Would you like a cup of tea?" my education and upbringing expressed themselves.

"Don't you have anything stronger?"

We had only drunk Chinese tea in the restaurant, I hadn't thought to order wine as I don't have the habit to drink it.

I keep a bottle of brandy for 'medical reasons' in the kitchen cupboard which I quickly hunted out.

"Will this do?"

"Yes, David, I'm sure that it will do, wonderfully".

She floated, (yes, floated seems the right way to describe it), she floated down onto my old sofa, (actually my dead grandma's sofa), and stretched languidly like a sleepy, giant cat.

"Bring the glasses and let's relax a little".

'Morning has Broken':

This time my alarm meditation did not wake me in the
middle of my best dream ever, it woke me long, long after
I had finished that one and melted into many, many others.

I awoke, fully expecting to find myself alone, that the
whole thing was just the distorted memory of a dream.

A beautiful, long, complicated, wonderful, superb dream
but now ready to face the cold lonely day type of dream.

But then again, if it really was a dream, why am I waking
up on the coach?

Why are my clothes scattered here and there? And what is
a pair of high heel pumps doing hanging around my living
room!

So it must be true then. Then again, if it was true then
where was ….

"Good morning David", she entered from my cubby hole
of a kitchen with a tray of coffee and toast, "you were still
sleeping so I invaded your kitchen. I hope that you don't
mind."

From that moment on my life became a miracle.

There she was, in the morning, in the evening, during the
weekends and holidays, always there, always available.

The Waking Dream:

I tried from time to time to ask her personal questions about herself and her life, but she always managed to wriggle out of the subject.

Of course, I could have pushed for some answers, I didn't even know whether she was an illegal immigrant from another country or a runaway bride or anything. The truth of the matter was, I didn't want to know.

She seemed to have neither friends nor family nor any wish or desire than to be with me.

The only strange things were; that she didn't want to travel, (illegal immigrant) and that she just HAD to be in bed and asleep by eleven o'clock, not only asleep mind you but not to be disturbed until six at the earliest.

There were times when I tried to take her out to a late film or a club but by ten p.m., she was begging me to bring her back home.

Also, on one occasion, I was showing off in a local Indian restaurant by ordering a hot vindaloo curry and felt really bad during the night.

I tried to wake her up, expecting a Florence Nightingale to pander to her wounded soldier but to my great surprise she looked at me in an totally shocked fashion.

She then started sobbing that I really, really must let her go back to sleep immediately or else it would 'be awful'.

So I reluctantly looked after myself while she thankfully returned to sleep.

We were happily watching the box one night when my perfect world began to fall to pieces.

I had noticed that one of my favourite films was to be shown in a late night slot and I was full of the expectation to share this jewel of British film comedy with my new woman, when she quietly reminded me that she needed to go to bed as it was nearly eleven o'clock.

The Nightmare Begins:

"But I want you to watch this with me, it's really good, I'm sure you'll like it".

"If you like it, David, then I'm sure that I will too."

"Then where's the problem?"

"But you know, I've got to be in bed, asleep for eleven."

"But you don't have to get up in the morning, I'm sure you can cope to stay up another couple of hours, just this once."

"But David, I can't". I could hear the panic in her voice, but I really couldn't understand why.

"It just doesn't make any sense, why do you 'just have to be 'in bed and asleep by eleven o'clock?"

"Because it's my job!" she blurted out, looking shocked and angry and hurt in turn by moment.

"What are you talking about?"

"I can't tell you."

"This is insane." I too was angry but also very confused. She shook her head and ran out of the room.

"Where are you going?"

"I've got to go to bed."

"You don't go anywhere until you explain to me what's going on?"

"David please, I'll tell you tomorrow, I promise but I've got to go to bed NOW."

"You go no-where until you explain to me this thing."

"David, please, I love you, but you've got to let me go to bed, I really, really must."

"Tell me what's going on." I was shouting now, I don't often lose it but when I start to go, I can go off really fast.

"Please, please David, it's time for me to go, please let me go."

She was sobbing, sobbing in my arms, the woman of my dreams was sobbing in my arms because I wouldn't let her go to bed at eleven o'clock.

The energy drained from my body, we held each other gently for a moment and then she slipped out, jumped into our bed, fully clothed and immediately fell asleep.

I started watching the film, but I had no stomach for it.

I returned to the bedroom and gently and carefully undressed her, but she didn't wake up – she was a very deep sleeper.

There she was, laying sleeping in my bed with a half-smile on her face – as usual.

The Fantastic Truth:

The next morning, I was already making coffee when she awake.

"David?" she knew that she was in trouble, that she would have to explain something this time.

She came into the living room as I entered with the coffee, she was wearing some old pyjamas of mine.

Her hair was sleep tangled and her eyes were still sticky, she should have looked sexy as hell, but I wasn't in any mood to be seduced by this very weird creature.

This very beautiful, but weird creature, that I had shared my life with these last weeks.

We both took our coffees and sat down in silence. I took a sip of mine.

"Well?" I opened up the discussion.

"David, I love you, please don't ask me to explain things".

"Why not?"

"Don't you love me?"

"What's that got to do with anything?"

"It's got everything to do with it. Do you love me?"

"Yes, I think I do".

"Then promise me one thing."

"What?"

"Don't ask me any questions."

"I can't, it's too weird, I've got to know."

"But if you knew, maybe you wouldn't love me anymore."

"I have no idea what you are talking about."

"Then please leave it that way."

I stopped for a moment, I considered what she was saying but the need to know was too strong, I just had to know, to understand.

"You have to tell me; you have to tell me now." This time it was her turn to stop.

She looked at me for a moment, took a big mouthful of hot coffee, too hot I would think from her reaction.

She swallowed the coffee, looking at me with eyes of a scared faun, (we've all seen Bambi, haven't we?).

"David, you call me the woman of your dreams."

"Yes, I believe that I saw you in a dream before we met. I know it sounds a bit daft."

"But it is not at all daft, it's true."

"What?"

"Yes, it's true, we met in your dream the night before we met on the bus, I looked for you."

"But it's not possible, it was just a coincidence or maybe I'm remembering it wrong now. Maybe I did have a sexy dream of a woman before I met you and now I've changed it to be you."

"No David, it was exactly like that, exactly like you remember, I was the woman in your dream that night and I looked and found you the next day."

"And exactly how did you manage to get into my dream?"

"Because that's my job David, my job is to enter into men's dreams.

Why do you think that I cannot travel too far? I have to stay in the same time zone.

Why do I have to be asleep by eleven o'clock? Because that's the hour that I start my shift."

"This is stupid, this is total rubbish, I don't believe it."

"I have no other explication for my strange behaviour David."

It was there that I let the subject drop, I had my work waiting for me.

I couldn't let this strange story be the cause for my being late, after all I was starting to be appreciated at work these last few weeks.

'Falling, falling, falling':

The day was a nightmare, I just couldn't concentrate. By four o'clock Bob felt the need to come down to my office.

"What's happening Dave?" he asked in a cheery voice. I knew that I must be in trouble, that was the cheery voice that leads to the unemployment line.

"I'm not feeling very well Bob".

"You're certainly not working very well today Dave."

"I know and I'll surely make up the late work tomorrow."

"Sure you will", he smiled and left. I translated his last phrase into 'You'd better' and prayed that I would.

I left the office as the clock struck; I dreaded going home but rushed in like the charge of the light brigade entering the valley of death.

She was there as usual, dinner was a silent affair, we didn't even try to make small talk. It was again over coffee that the mornings' discussion was restarted.

"Are you serious about what you said this morning?"

"David, please do we have to talk about it?"

"Can you please answer my question."

"David, I love you."

"That does not answer the question."

"Yes, yes what I told you this morning is true. I know it must be very, very hard for you to believe me but that is what I do, that is my life's task."

"What, to go into men's dreams and to make love to them?"

"David, these men are lost and sad and lonely. They need something, something that might help them to feel better about themselves and then maybe, just maybe, that will help them be more successful in their waking lives."

"You are serious, aren't you?"

"David, you know that I love you."

It was her constant referring to her love for me that convinced me that she was telling the truth.

I don't know that much about people and their behaviour, even less when it comes to women but when someone keeps telling you that they love then you can bet your last shilling that they've slept with someone else.

My disbelief twisted magically into rage and disgust.

"Every night, here in our bed, sleeping next to me, you go to other men and have sex with them?"

I knew that I was losing it, the tone of my voice became harder, the volume was increasing.

"David, it's not like that."

I didn't care anymore, I just wanted to hurt her.

"You're nothing but a cheap prostitute, just a common whore."

"David, I love you. I don't take anything for what I do. What I do, I do for love."

She shouldn't have said that, she really, really shouldn't have.

"Oh yes, you have sex with them for love and yet I'm the man that you love, am I understanding right?"

"No, no, that isn't at all what I meant," she was crying now but I really didn't care, she was just a slut and she had used me.

Lived with me for weeks, never once paying for anything, a real kept woman in every sense of the term.

"You disgust me."

"Please, please, please don't say that." Suddenly she stopped.

"What now?" I couldn't help but ask.

"What time is it?"

"What does it matter what time it is?"

"It must be eleven o'clock."

"So?"

"I have to go to bed, to go to sleep, to go to work."

"Oh no you don't."

"David, please, I have to."

There are times, not that it makes me proud to admit it but there are times when knowing just where to put the knife to hurt someone the maximum brings a humongous pleasure.

This sleeping business was her Achilles' heel, it was the only thing that seemed important to her and I had the power to stop her doing it.

"No," my voice was suddenly deadly calm, "no, I don't think so, not tonight at least. Tonight, you can take a night off."

"No David, I can't," there was panic in her voice, "I have to, I really do".

"Yes, you've just got to go and sleep with men."

"Yes, that's it, that's what I do and if you can't accept that then I'll have to leave you."

"You'll leave me!", I was screaming now, "just like that? You think that it's normal to think that I would accept for you to stay and carry on doing that?"

The craziness of what I was saying totally escaped me at the time, I was too angry and too hurt to think further than the next sentence or action.

"David, please, please let me stay with you."

"No problem," I could see the hope raising in her eyes because she was too trusting to expect just how nasty I can be when pushed, "just as long as you only sleep during the day".

"I can't, I can't."

"Oh we'll see about that. Tonight will be the first test."

"What are you saying?"

"Tonight you don't sleep and I'm staying up to keep watch."

"David, please, you have to let me go to sleep, to do my work, you have to."

"So that some randy, old sod can have his tasty bit of stuff?"

"Please, don't say it like that," but I did and I kept saying it, over and over in a dozen different ways.

She pleaded, she begged, she cried but it was like talking to a stone, I just couldn't let it go, I just had to win.

What difference would it make to the balance of the world if one more or one less miserable sod was to have an erotic dream this night?

What difference when it was costing me my very soul?

I just wanted her to prove that I was more important than any other man on earth but she wouldn't, she just kept on and on and on, how she must do her job, having virtual sex with some stranger.

The hours wore on, she stopped asking me, there she sat, in a corner of the room, back against the two walls, cold, weary, miserable.

She did not dare to go to sleep, she well knew in the state I was in that I would only shout at her until she woke up.

"David?"

"Yes?"

"Your work."

"What about it?"

"You need to sleep or you'll not be able to work properly. I know how important your work is to you."

Almost any other person in the same situation would have used that as a ploy to get their own way but not her.

She was much too naïve and innocent to try and trick or manipulate me.

"What do you care?"

"You know I do," and of course I did.

"And if I go to sleep, so will you?"

"You know that I will," she answered very softly.

We undressed in silence, my rage had exhausted me, but I was still feeling angry with her. "Then it's finished I guess."

"But it is only in a dream."

"Like I was only in a dream?"

"That's how I first met you."

A New Dream:

Miracles can happen with prayers, through wishing, through desire or just spontaneously or any combination these or other reasons.

I know not from where this miracle came but it did, an incredible flash of lightening out of a clear blue sky, unexpected as desert rain.

You see, after all this time, blocked by my own hopeless sense of lack of worth, I had not listened, I had not heard, I had not reached the most obvious of conclusions.

"It's okay, you go to sleep, do your job and I'll be here to hold you in the morning." She was too beaten by the evenings' war to integrate what I was saying.

"I'm sorry, I'm really, really sorry. I'll never question again your need to do what you have to do with any other man."

"Why have you changed your mind?" I could see that she desperately wanted to believe me, but she was having a problem trusting this, all too radical change.

"Because I was too stupid to understand before and now I think I do."

"What do you understand now David?" she asked quietly.

"You met me in a dream and the next day you came to find me. It's obvious…..

….. I am the MAN of YOUR dreams."

Crying for the Raindrops

This is one of the songs that I wrote during my first year at Aston University.

It was a time of relative calm; my studies were within my capabilities, I had friendly growing relationships with some of the students on my 'floor' of our university residence, 'Lawrence Tower', (my best friends Graham and Kevin came from there), and my young-ado relationship with Debbie was fading away.

In fact, I had much time to hang around in my two by three metre 'cell' of a room and dream.

This song was one of the fruits of these lost moments.

Crying for the Raindrops

Sitting in the silence of my lonely little room
Staring out the window, as I watch the evening gloom
Thinking of the places and all the things I've done
Looking at the faces of the people I've become.

Waiting for the meaning, I'm just listening for a word
Asking, 'Am I dreaming?', 'Was that someone I just heard?'
List'ning to the footfall, but unable to turn 'round.
Standing in the cold hall, 'so at last, have I been found?'

Crying for the raindrops is a message to the night
Because she hides her face, we all think it is right
But who will ask the questions?
"What's happened to the moon?"
"Is she hiding in the star-ways?"
And, "Will she come out soon?"

Sharing at the silence of this noisy, awful room
Staring at the window as we catch reflected gloom
Going to the places to undo the things we've done
Erasing the sad faces of the people we've become.

Giving up the meaning, for us, love's become the word
Floating like we're dreaming, and we hope they too have heard
Smiling at our footfall, 'cause the word has turned us round
Kissing in the cool hall, I was lost but now I'm found.

Crying for the raindrops was a message for the night
Because she hid her face, we all thought it was right
We dared to ask the question.
"What's happened to the moon?"
"She was hiding in the star-ways"
But now she'll come out soon.

Far from Home

This story was written as a birthday present for my wife.

1995, I had just begun my second university studies at the University of Lausanne.

I had very little money and was fighting with the challenge of studying at university level, in a language that I hardly understood.

I also had little time alone, as my then girlfriend and I shared a weird studio apartment above a bar – nightclub. (Le Lapin Vert).

So, I thought to write this story for her.

-Which I wrote in a pocket notebook, during the short journeys of about 10 minutes, on the metro, (subway), between the terminus, (Flon) and the university stop, (Dorigny).

Writing a story in chunks of ten minutes on a busy metro was an interesting exercise.

Far from Home

The ship lurched, and Captain Raymond spun the wheel hard to starboard.

Mountainous waves, erupting from the angry churning sea, lashing the bridge with its furious spray.

She, mad with some inner rage, had found this sorry excuse of a vessel on which to spend her pain.

The veteran mariner twisted his mouth into a gritty smile.

"Okay you wicked bitch, I don't know what's got your goat this time, but you ain't gonna rid o' me yet."

The boat, a lonely, single car on a crazy fairground ride, twisted, pitched and rolled, through the tortured, tormented sea.   Which was, in fact, the Atlantic Ocean.

And while this noisy outer battle raged, setting his wits and trawler against the foaming foe, Raymond fought to comprehend the reason for this sudden onslaught.

After all, the meteo was clear, nothing was forecast, nor was there wind or rain.

One moment she was calm and steady as anything, and then, wham! out of the blue, this.
He shook his white flecked beard and spun the wheel.

The world was flat.

Every movement exhausted, inner and outer.

Hardly a wave or a ripple disturbed the steady, green waters' surface. All emotion weary and spent.

To say that the sea or Raymond were now calm would be inaccurate, for that would intimate a sense of peacefulness, where-as, in truth, emptiness, would be a much closer description.

In fact, Raymond was troubled. His long years of experience at sea had taught him all there was to know of this unpredictable females' capricious moods. - Or so he thought!

A tempest without either wind nor storms, this was not within his knowledge or experience.

- And now this.

The creature was very light, soft, gelatinous and vaguely phosphorescent. Two fine, horn-like structures protruded, from where, on a normal fish, would have been its eyes.

Presumably, there had been some form of eyes attached but had failed to weather the journey from whence it came.

The ship board radio crackled the response he had been waiting for.

"Major seismic disturbance registered in your vicinity, force 10 or better."

"Or better?", Raymond laughed quietly to himself.

"Concerning unusual specimens", the ethereal voice continued, "entire catch has been purchased by the Oceanic Institute of Florida. Confirm temperature and water level, then seal hatch."

Raymond wondered what other deep-sea monstrosities the sub-aquatic earthquake had propelled to the surface, and that he had unintentionally scooped up into his rusty hold.

The ship was designed to land the fish alive, could any of these science fiction inspired creatures have survived the trauma of their deep ocean eviction, to continue, 'vivant', alive, journeying towards the sun?

Speculate as he might, he was exhausted from his previous efforts, and was only too happy to check on the water and the temperature, before extending himself the full length of his bunk and descending into his own sweet oblivion

Joshua O'Brian smiled, an event precious and rare. Precious, firstly because of its rarity, but also because of the dazzling brilliant contrast of his pearly white teeth gleaming through his onyx black face.

And yes, quite rare, because of late there had been little to smile about.

His hair featured the usual tight woolly negro curls, but the deep, rich copper hue, singled him out as belonging to a heritage ever so slightly different from the norm.

Where-as, his name, that left no question as to his genealogy.

Joshua's mother Hannah was a classic negress of the deep south. The great, granddaughter of plantation slaves, she had been well taught to accept the injustices of life with a shrug, a smile and a deep sigh that resonated from somewhere deep within her more than ample breasts.

The poverty and punishments of existence had augmented with the passing years, as her father had lost his job with the closing of the cotton mill and taken up a new career with the bottle.

And yet life could still be sweet, with church on Sundays, and swimming in the brook, and Thanks-Givings and helping with the cooking for the Henry Lees', and even, once in a while, a bright new hat.

David O'Brian was something else again, a short wild Irish-American, whose pioneering family, escaping poverty and starvation on the 'Emerald Isle' had fought and married their way into the respectable New England society.

David, named prophetically after his great-grandfather, Davy O'Brian, was a rebel and a fighter. His sharp wit, and even sharper tongue led him constantly into situations dangerous and violent.

Only his family's power and prestige kept him out of prison and in one college or other.

Eventually, much to his family's surprise and satisfaction he graduated law, phi-beta-capa. And when he decided to remove himself from the restrictive confines of the oppressively, structured New England society, their joy, (albeit unexpressed), was complete.

David O'Brian set himself up a law practice in a little town in South Carolina.   Fighting for civil rights and against anything that he could target to vent a frustration that came from somewhere deep within the O'Brian psyche.

Although he was tolerated, even respected by many factions of both the black and white communities, he was never accepted by either.

By the time that sweet, young Hannah took him to herself, people had already begun to comment on an increasing wildness in his manner of action and speech, and the faint tang of whisky on his breath.

Joshua was always slated to be an outcast. - Both within and without of his family.

His father was neither physically violent nor an unreasonable disciplinarian, he was even often quite gay and humorous, but then there were also many days when silence was the rule, and nobody spoke.

Joshua even remembered one particular time, when nobody broke the fragile silence for more than a whole week.

It began on a Tuesday, continued over one Sunday, and threatened to continue past another. When, all of a sudden, things changed, and they all had a wonderful party on the Saturday night.

Whether this was all due to the whisky, or was more a real expression of his fathers' inner process, was a question that he often asked himself in later life.

Hannah was always warm and caring, a classic mother.

Always available, someone who was always the same, always solid, stable, soft, secure.

To whom one could express any and everything, no idea or emotion was too extreme, no sentiment unacceptable.

Without interruption or criticism, she would quietly sit and listen to any and every problem that he would care to speak of.

"Yes, life's like that honey. Here, I've just baked a fresh pecan pie, it'll make you feel better".

And so it did. Little Joshua became Big Joshua, and all the answers to his problems came on a plate.

And what were his problems?

Evidently, being a half/half in that place at that time wasn't easy.

Rejected by both black and white communities, which was even further exacerbated by his connection to the 'wild Irish', as David O'Brian was, not so kindly, known within this region.

With his weird coloured hair and increasingly rotund
shape, he was an easy figure of fun. And children being
children, they surely didn't miss such a wonderful
opportunity.

Being an-only child, Joshua spent much time sitting out
the hot summers, in and around the local creek,
doing a lot of not much. (Other that is, than keeping cool).

By the time of his ninth birthday, he had begun to become quite fascinated by the only community that hadn't hitherto rejected him - the aquatic community of this watery world.

Not being unduly unintelligent, Joshua plunged himself into this underwater oasis.

Only to emerge 15 years later as a fully accredited marine biologist.

He had shed his excess pounds by replacing his sublimated oral gratification with an excessive intellectual drive, which gave him both the image and self-image of a successful, valued member of the scientific community.

Before, during and after this period, he had had and would have, his fair share of romantic and sexual encounters. All of which followed the same, well defined path.

He would meet a woman, seduce her with his soft, gentle ways and above average good looks.

Having fixed her with a sexual attention rarely, if ever found in a man of his age, at the time, only then to lose her over the longer term as she was forced to realise that it was totally impossible to make any real emotional connection with him.

The endings were many and varied, depending on the make-up of the woman and therefore the details of how the couple functioned.

The one and only constant was that there were endings and Joshua, once again would find himself alone.

Worse, he had no more contact with his parents after a particularly violent row with his father.

Watching other couples come together, marry, buy houses, have kids and raise families, he found himself becoming more and more bitter in his solitude.

Ranting at the unforgiving ghosts that had somehow managed to seep into his life, like a sour, lingering odour, who knows from where, but still here, and forever poisoning the environment.

Yes, it was also true, that from time to time, he took a little of his fathers' medicament, but never too much - after all, he had his work.

But today, here was possibly the find of the century. A unique opportunity to examine fresh flora and fauna from the very depths of the ocean.

And maybe, just maybe, he'd find something still alive.

For the past 24 hours he'd not stopped, neither to sleep, nor to eat more than the odd candy bar from the machine at the end of the hall.

His assistants had sent out for pizza and slept some hours each on the folding camp bed. - The one that he kept in the back store for those nights when he preferred to stay in the Institute, rather than return home to his empty apartment.

Joshua couldn't sleep; he needed a cooling plant, pressurised tanks, special lighting, video cameras, the list seemed unending.

If, if only there could be something still alive, and if he could keep it alive long enough to make a decent study, that would be something.

To publish the definitive paper on deep see marine life, fame, research grants, who knows what doors it might open.

"Dr. O'Brien, she's here, do you want to come and take a look?"

Stupid question, the boat had arrived with possibly the most important cargo ever, and, 'did he want to take a look?'

On passing, he took a final quick look at the wide gauge pump, to check that it was (still) calibrated to function at its lowest setting.

She was an ugly old tub, well rusted, peeling paint, foul smelling.

"Welcome aboard Captain", the old mariner was pleased to welcome the red eyed biologist. And well he might, the Institute would pay well for this particular catch, very well indeed.

Joshua smiled, but the tight polite smile, which had become his habit of late.

"I trust that you have followed all my instructions carefully."

Raymond felt an icy blast of memory thrust him back into the dark days of his apprenticeship on board the "Grimsby Queen".

As a lowly cabin boy the first mate was next to God, and when-ever he asked if "all my instructions have been carried out", it meant that someone was in a bad mood, and someone else, someone small and defenceless was about to be beaten up.

All that was lacking was the pretext, but that would be quickly rectified.

And now, even this half smiling, American negro looked similar.

"Well?"

"Yes captain, sorry captain, of course, of course."

Then, like an overstretched elastic, time sprang back into place, forty years passed in an instant.

"Yes sir, of course I've followed your instructions. All the conditions have been followed as required."

"Good", and with that, the doctor turned abruptly away to politely bully the engineers, as they carefully unloaded his precious cargo.

It was calm and dark when he awoke. Looking at his watch he was slightly surprised to notice that it was 2 o'clock in the morning.

He had succumbed to his body's demands around midday.

The ship's hold had been gently suctioned clean, and its contents deposited in a vast array of assorted glass tanks.

In fact, every tank of any sort, that passed a minimum size, within a ten-mile radius, that could be borrowed or bought, had been transported here in the last 24 hours.

The temperature had been lowered to near zero and the lights regulated to the barest minimum. Pumps were pressurising the tanks well beyond any manufacturer's specification.

It was in this chilly, twilight world that he had cloistered himself.

Where almost immediately, on the release of the tension of realizing this immense project, his nervous energy had dissipated.

It was only by an enormous effort of will that he managed to get to his cot before falling deeply asleep.

Maybe it was the cold, but also definitely a function of the vast quantities of coffee that he had consumed over the past hours, that, at 2 a.m., had forced him to re-emerge into the waking world.

He unlocked the door of the lab, confirmed that the blackout material still protected the inside from the bright exterior corridor lights and carefully left to do the 'necessary'.

Ten minutes later he was back, washed and toileted. Then a fresh pot of coffee was put on, and it's comforting aroma and the gentle sounds of the percolator soon filled the darkened room.

The first quick circuit took little more than a half hour.

The tanks were all pre-numbered, and there was a separate notebook for each, so all that he had to do was to walk to each tank in turn, take its notebook and mark down his preliminary observations about its contents.

Of course, he could have left his assistants to do this, but he was much too greedy, lest one of them discovered the 'living proof that he craved.

The pumps he long since fulfilled their function, as had the coffee percolator. The room was silent. Most of the tanks showed no signs of life what-so-ever.

And amongst the others that did contain the live specimens, for which so much effort had been made, nothing within them could have been considered as a major scientific find.

All had hither to been seen, classified, even videotaped during many of the well-publicised and documented bio-sphere descents of the past years.

Of course, having such specimens, alive and on the surface could only advance the wealth of scientific knowledge within the subject, but nothing of earth-shattering significance.

It was then that he thought he saw a movement, a movement in one of the tanks he had concluded as empty.

'So', he smiled to himself, 'something has been trying to hide itself from me'.

He moved quickly to the tank in question. There was still a small cloud of minute fine particles in the water, fine sediment stirred up by something emerging from under, that had not quite yet returned to their bed.

Of course it had to be small, or else it could not have escaped his notice, during his first tour. He peered into the tank, should he dare to use his pocket flashlight and risk blinding the poor creature?

But wait, yes, there was something, there, moving, moving towards him.

Its motion was very, very slow, he held his breath.

Something like an upturned squid, a thin fishlike tail, but atop of which, it sported a mass of fine golden fronds.

Maybe it was a weird form of carnivorous plant.

It couldn't be a cross, and yet it definitely had a totally banal aquatic tail.

As it continued to approach, he had the weirdest fancy, it seemed, that under the fronds, it was propelling itself, with all things, a pair of arms!

He bent down to have a closer look, but as he approached the glass, the creature stopped.

'Could it be aware of my presence?', Joshua wondered to himself.

He backed away slightly, and the creature resumed its slow advance.

Suddenly a bright light flashed on and off.

The   creature, startled, reacted instantly and disappeared.

Joshua was intrigued, surprised and furious all at the same time.

The flashing light was from the telephone, he had switched it to mute mode, so not to be disturbed, forgetting that on such a setting, the ringer activated a small flashing light.

Particularly intense in these circumstances.

The night watchman's solicitous inquiry as to his general well-being received a very rude response!

It took the creature a full five minutes to venture out again. Joshua had dragged a chair over and was patiently watching it approach.

He was split between the idea of unpacking the video equipment to record the moment, and the urgent desire to see clearly what the creature was.

It approached closer and closer, yes, they surely looked like arms. It reached the impenetrable barrier and bumped straight into it!

'Not much glass where you come from, I bet', he thought.

The creature jerked back, the "arms" came up and parted the fronds ...

The shock was total!

She was beautiful.

Of course her eyes where huge and of the very, very palest blue, and her skin was of the purest coral white, but still, (or more than likely because of these characteristics), she was incredibly, incredibly beautiful.

Yes, he was shocked, but not only he, her eyes, already enormous by human standards, opened, wider and wider.

It was then that she did something, so totally, utterly unexpected, that he nearly fell off of his chair.

 - She smiled.

Imagine, being thrust by the most violent force, into a totally strange land, and then being confronted to a giant, the equivalent of 70 metres high.

 - And then to smile.

And what a smile, the most perfect combination of a sweet innocent child, coupled with the sensuous sexuality of a young woman.

And then, something even more surprising happened ...

Joshua O'Brian smiled, an event precious and rare.

Love and lust are two experiences which, in our modern society, when discussing the relationship between two adults, often become confused and inter changeable.

Joshua O'Brian was in love.

Two creatures from two totally different worlds of the same planet. Here, separated by a glass wall, necessary for reasons of survival.

Her watery, pressurised world, his too, watery and pressurised, but only in the figurative sense.

Two beings, completely alone, through different circumstances of the same fate. Meeting here, and still so separate.

And yet, they had connected, the link was real and sound.

This was not a tragic star-crossed love that one might read of in an old novel, fractured by family feuds, parted by political disputes or any other form of frustrated fraternity.

This was not a love of pain and suffering.

Does one suffer before a great painting, a poem or a piece of music?

A snow flake, a soap bubble, a sun beam, fragile moments in time. Ungraspable, unique, perfect.

It is itself, and that is everything.

Joshua was in love, blissfully, ecstatically in love.

But how to better communicate his love? Here she was, smiling at him, to him, with him, but there must be something more. What to do?

What expression?   How to proceed?

Joshua picked up the phone and dialled a number.

It was cold this morning. Captain Raymond pulled at the wheel and corrected the ship's course by the one or two points necessary to bring her over the target area.

He looked up and over at his two mismatched passengers and spoke to the taller of the two.

"Well Doctor, I think that that's about it."

"I trust that you are correct."

Over the past few days Raymond had come to accept the cold, formal tone, for what it was - a tone, no more, no less. No more a reason to relive has shamed youth.

"It's as good as we're gonna get."

Joshua turned to his love, there was so much that he wanted to say, so much more that he'd have liked to express.

But he had spoken; spoken for hours and hours.

He had sat before her glass palace, and he had poured his heart out.

And all the time she had loved him, while he had laughed and cried, with the stories of his past, of his relationships, his exhausted hopes and broken dreams.

And she had smiled, sometimes she had seemed shocked, even hurt, when his rage had bubbled over.

Years of suppressed tolerance, boiling forth in the white-hot lava of brimming emotion, but most of the time she smiled.

Once or twice he thought that maybe she was laughing, when he recounted a happy or particularly amusing episode.

And so, now it was time. Time to send her home, home to her own kind, her own people.

They disconnected the pumps. Joshua made swimming motions with his arms, maybe she understood, maybe not.

He bent close and kissed the ice-cold glass.

Raymond activated the mini-crane, and she swung up and over the boat's rail.

They had estimated that the weight of the tank would be more than sufficient to force its direct descent, and that well before it reached the bottom, the pressure would break open the tank's glass panels, and release its precious cargo.

Raymond stopped the arm with the tank just touching the water, he nodded to the complicated American, who gently touched the release switch - and she was gone.

There was a slight breeze that morning, and Raymond fancied that maybe a little sea spray had hit them both in the eyes at the same time.

He turned once again, towards Joshua, the black hands with pink palms were wiping the 'spray' from his eyes as he spoke.

"I think maybe it's time that I went home."

No Distance

This collection of songs and poems are amongst the fruit of my stay at the Findhorn spiritual community in Scotland, 1992 – 3.

During a long moment of sexual and relationship lack, I had a very short, intense and yet frustrating contact with a German woman, name of Ziggy.

To deal with my emotional torment, (and frustration!), I plunged myself into a series of poems.

For this work, I have allowed myself the artistic licence to complete and enrich them with other pieces that I wrote (mostly) during the same period.

No Distance

Nightmare

Everywhere
Suddenly
There
Grabbing
For Me
Arms

Reaching
Like
Creeping
Zombie
Death

I Duck
To Avoid
Their Touch
And Run

Into Her
She
Who Appears
Most Often

Golden Image
Of Wond'ress Desires

I Touch

Her
My Body
Thrills

"I'm Only
A Projection
Of Your
Frustrated
Affection

Face
The Reality
I'm But
A Fantasy"

She Smiles
Sweetly
And Disappears
Out
From
My Arms

For
The Millionth Time
It Is
An Endless Twilight

And On
They Come
Those
I
Love, Hate, Fear, Respect

"We Are But Mirrors"
They Reflect
And Change Into
Fantastic Faces
Of Me

A Huge Metal Coffin
Looms Up
Before Me

I Enter Its Tomb
Like Silence

Inside There Is
A Bed

Untidy
Yet Inviting

I Throw Off My Clothes
And Slide Under The Covers

'What Worse Could Happen Now?'
I Ask Myself

'I Suppose I Could Have A Nightmare.'

The Room Where I live.

There is a room
Inside
I live.

It is warm
Safe
Unthreatening

I watch
Through a
Picture window

Life
Unfolding
Dangerous

Sealed
Inside
Safety

Warm
Dry
Comfortable

Something
Pricks
My Psyche

I don my jacket
Unseal the door
And start
To live
Again.

Floating

Floating, floating through the years of my life
Cushioned in my sleep
Dreamtime very deep
Nothing else to do but count the sheep.

'Till there was you
Tugging at my arm
I know dear
You don't mean no harm
But you tore
This dreamer from his sleep
Here I am lying in a heap

Floating ….

'Till there was you
Now I'm wide awake
So is this thing
Just a big mistake?
In this life
There never was a cert
I'm not sure
That won't get hurt.

Floating ….

'Till there was you
Brought me back to life
I can feel
All trouble and all strife.
Is it worth
All this re-found pain?
To return
And fall in love again?

Floating ….

'Till there was you
Op'ning up my heart
My whole life's
Got a brand-new start
You're a dream
Suddenly come true
I'm complete
Now that I have you

Floating, floating through the years of my life
Drifting in the spas
Evenings in the bars
Nothing else to do but count the stars.

They move and Dance

They move and Dance
In and Out of His
Consciousness

The Girls
Mysterious Distant
Them

One Special She
Begins to Stand Out

She
Most Beautiful
Of Course
Not for You

Suddenly She is
Here
Poor awkward
You

Mumble and Study
Important Shoes

Gently Waiting
She stands

And then is Gone

Relief pours Through tensioned Veins

The Meetings Continue

Shyness Shackles Speech

And then It Happens
The Miracle

He sees Her afar
And then Is
… by Her

And eyes Meet
He speaks "Hello"

The Gentle Touch

The Gentle Touch
Thrills

Electric

Immense
Pain of Partings

Emptiness
In Waiting

Rapture
Of Return

I See
You
Serious, Distant, Thoughtful
Clouded, Countenance

I Stretch Outwards
To you
Aching

And then
You
See
Me

Brilliant Dazzling Shining Sunlight
Your Smile Erupts

And again
The gentle Touches

Of
A Look
A Word
A Flower

Your hand
Brushing Mine

Sweet, Gentle, Wonder

Innocence
Yet Hidden

Deep Within Secret Longings

The Dragon Stirs

The Dragon Stirs

Fascinated
Restrained
The Horse
Excited

Is Held
Within the
Confines of
The Starting Gate

- Hot to Trot
You
Self Consciously, Mechanically, Fold
Your Clothes

"And They're Off!"

Helter Skelter
They Race

Neck and Neck

The Riders
Driven
By the Frantic Charging
Of the Semi-Wild Beasts

Almost Beyond
Their Control

The goal is
Clear and Approaching Fast

The panting Efforts of the Mounts
As they Force Themselves
Ever Faster Forward

They are now
Thrusting
Towards
The Final Finish

Sweet Sweat
Pours from their Bodies

And it is

…. Over

Spent yet Energised
They Retire

The Summer's Days

The Summer's Days
Loll
Into Quiet
Contentment

Daily Dosed
With Gentle
Wonders

Eternal Bliss
Continues

NOT

The Refreshing Cooling Breeze Chills
Shivers of
Apprehension
Creep Threateningly
Up my Spine

The Sun becomes Distant
Faint clouds of Concern
Drift into view

The Wind Whispers a Warning Word
I
Hear Your Words

Goodbye Sunshine

But Why Must You Leave?

"It is Time"

The heavy Clouds
Close over my Heart

It is Cold In my World

It
Starts to Rain ....

When Did We ?

When Did We Two Fall
Into Love?

Nice, Friendly Souls
Not Really Attracted

But Gentle Caring and Supportive

Never Electric Vivid
Deep Throated Sudden

LOVE

But A
Touch
Lingered A
Kiss
Meaningful A
Hug That Almost
Meant More Than
Friend

Do I Love Thee?

Of Course I Do

But Yet Only As
The Beautiful Butterfly You Are

Brush My Lips
With Gossamer Wings

As On You Fly

And I Will Kiss
With All My Heart

My Love Goodbye

On the Cross of Love

Hanging out
On the
Cross of Love

Higher, Separate, Alone

This
Is my own Cross
I
Built it, Carried it, Raised it

This
Is my own Cross
I
Mount myself upon it
Spread myself against it
Strap myself tight to it

This
Is my own Cross
My thought crystal clear
My heart loves it dear
My body aches

This
Is my own Cross

Why have I
Forsaken me?

Time

Time, Friend Hast Returned You to Me

Entwined
Through Quiet Gentle Years

Supporting One
Then the Other

Never more the
Distance of Separation

Root and Branch
We are
One

Your Velvet Hand on my Cheek

A Constant Reminder Of
Our soft Gentle Love

The Years Have been Kind

Yet Now
Again
It is Time

And
You must Travel Your Only Path

Back to Home

Do Not Look Back
There is Nothing to See

A Soft
Gentle Sadness
Mantles My Form

I
Thank-you
For Your Love

There Is
No Distance

Nylons in the Sink

And now for a little light relief.

During one of my long evenings with my friends Graham and Kevin, (and maybe Helmut, a German exchange student, pianist and musician), I was showing off, just a little bit.

(Final year at Aston University, circa 1979, about 22 years old).

I was saying that I could write a poem or a song on almost any subject, and in any tone.

So they give me two challenges; to write something humorous firstly about death, and secondly about breaking up.

The death song was about grave robbing – "Death Warms me Up", and the song about breaking up, is 'Nylons in the Sink'.

Nylons in the Sink

Oh, what happened to my lady and what am I to do?
She used to be my only, but now for only you.
A girl of many assets, as the daytime brings
A lass surprising faultless, except for these few things.

Oh, there's just the little problem of the nylons in the sink
And the hankies from the laundry, that somehow come back pink
There's just the little problem of the lipstick on my cuff
And how did my lost shammy, become a powder-puff?

Oh, what happened to my lady ….?

There's just the little problem of the way she'd tidy 'round
How could one lose a golf set, weighing over thirty pounds?
There's just the little problem of the grape and honey diet
I'm not that narrow minded, but did she have to fry it?

Oh, what happened to my lady ….?

There's just the little problem of the way she parks the car
Which side one should embark from, both curbs are just as far
There's just the problem of the pets she thought to choose
It's not that I hate goats but, it's eaten my best shoes.

Oh, what happened to my lady ….?

There's just the little problem of the things that she got sold
And was the lounge the place for a Louis quinze commode?
There's just the little problem with the girlfriends she'd invite
The soirées started purr-fect, but cats will always fight.

Oh, what happened to my lady ….?

There's just the little problem of time she'd take to dress
'Cus to arrive the next day, is failing to impress.
There's just the little problem when her mother came to stay
She understood, 'please come in', but not quite 'go away'.

Oh, what happened to my lady and what am I to do?
She used to be my only, but now for only you.
A girl of many assets, as the daytime brings
Surprisingly I'm missing her and mostly for those things.

I saw tomorrow crying

This is one of my older contributions.

When at the Collegiate Grammar School in Blackpool, during my 15th year, I wrote a story for an English composition exercise.

Several years later I joined an amateur youth theatre group, (strangely run by the same English teacher), the Fylde Youth Theatre, (I think).

One of the other young actors, (Steve?), was interested in making 8mm films.

So, in 1974, (I was 17), we embarked on a project to make ourselves a film.

For this, I took my short story and expanded it into a series of poems and songs.

The beautiful, talented, (and very attractive), Ann Lloyd accepted to be my love interest. (I was the writer, co-editor, special effects creator and leading man).

This song was the at the end of the film.

I saw tomorrow crying

I saw tomorrow crying
So I stopped to ease her pain
And heard the wind a sighing
"I'll never sing again."
I felt the day a-breaking
Its heart all broken wide
The rain was crying softly
And again, the wind she sighed.

The dreamer sharply wakened
Finds this world unreal
A hundred years of sleep-dust
Has clogged her spinning wheel
The world cannot be honest
Its existence is the lie
The lie will keep revolving
And the world will often cry

I saw tomorrow crying
So I stopped to ease her pain
And heard the wind a sighing
"I'll never sing again."

The Ugly Barren Fruit Tree

This was the second story written during my shamanic nature workshop.

I initially wrote it in French, which is most unusual for me, but I wanted to share it with the rest of the participants.

The story itself came out of an exercise in linking oneself energetically to a tree. The tale is almost an obvious extension of that experience.

The Ugly Barren Fruit Tree

Once there was an enormous storm and a great bird was blown 1,000s of miles off course and to the north. Hence, she found herself in a place where she had absolutely no business to be.

Now this bird, which was flying over a newly planted apple orchard had been eating a very rare fruit, from a very rare tree and a pip from that tree found itself in the rich prepared soil of the orchard and took root.

The next spring, the young son of the owner of the orchard, passing amongst the young apple trees noticed a small sprig with most unusual shaped leaves.

'How pretty', he said to himself, 'I wonder what it could be.'

He asked his father if he could come and enlighten him as to the nature of the tree.

His father came but sadly had to admit that he had never seen the like before.

"But it doesn't matter, I'll just pull it out and that will be that".

"No, please", pleaded the son, "you always said that I should take an interest in the trees, please, please leave me this tree to look after".

The boy's mother, intrigued by the demand of her son to know the name of a tree had come and joined the discussion.

"Why not leave him his tree, it does no harm to the other trees and he needs to start interesting himself in the orchard sooner or later?"

And so it was agreed that the little sapling of unknown origin was given over to the son of the owner, as his own tree.

And straight away he began to look after it.

Throughout the summer months he would make sure that it was kept well-watered.

If the cows were allowed to graze in the orchard, that his tree was well protected.

And in the winter months, that the base was covered by layers of old leaves, hay and pine branches and the little trunk was wrapped in old clothes and protected by an old tarpaulin.

"What makes you think that that is the way to look after the tree?" queried his parents.

"Don't know", answered the young man.

"Surely someone must have told you what to do, you seem very sure of what it needs."

"Don't know", he repeated and ran off.

Of course he did know but he couldn't tell anyone. He knew because the tree told him what it needed.

The boy didn't understand just how the tree communicated its needs to him but he just knew what he had to do and that the information came from the tree.

And so the years passed, quite quickly the apple trees started to produce their fruit and year after year the crops increased.

True, the boy's tree continued to grow and flourish, but it produced nothing, not even a flower.

From time to time, the boy's father asked if it was really worthwhile to keep the tree, which was getting quite big and would soon start to block the light from the other trees but the young man reminded him of the promise that the tree was given to him and that no-one had the right to touch it.

At the tender age of fourteen, he fell in love for the very first time.

The habit of the village boys was to go to their favourite tree and carve their name and the name of their beloved on the tree.

- A message that would live 'forever'.

And so, full of loves' first flush, he advanced towards the tree, knife at the ready, to inscribe, forever, the names of the young lovers.

His blade touched the bark, but his arm resisted, 'no, it was not the way, not this time, not with this tree'.

As a token of her love, she had given to him a personal object. He had tied her red ribbon around his wrist.

Soon after, one could notice, looking into the orchard, one of the trees, decorated with a pretty, red ribbon on one of its branches, dancing in the breeze.

In the winter of the young man's seventeenth year his father caught a chill.

With very little money to buy medication or pay for doctor's visits the brave man fought through the long, hard winter and the whole of the next summer.

But winter hit him hard a second time and spring came around without his warm smile and sunny disposition.

The day of the funeral was bleak and cold.

The ground was hard from the frost and the sorrow of the day.

The priest spoke of a man loved and respected by his friends and his community.

And of how his loved ones would miss him but rejoice in his ascension to heaven.

They all left, and the young man found himself alone with his grief.

The rest of the family seemed to find solace together, but he felt no space or contact to feel his loss.

His tree had grown with the years, taller, thicker, broader. Still fruitless but healthy and sturdy.

His hands stretched out in need of contact and comfort.

The bark was rough and rugged, yet warm and welcoming.

He hugged the bough with all his force and the tears flooded out like a summer storm.

His friend; staunch, straight and solid, supported him through his grief.

After the storm, the calm, exhausted, he folded himself between the roots of his wooden twin and fell asleep.

The next morning, on awakening, he reasoned to himself that the tree had accepted his grief, so the only thing to do, was to remove the black armband for his arm and tie it to a branch.

****

And so the tradition began: for each major event, good or bad, in the man's life, a ribbon, red for celebration, black for mourning would decorate the tree:

The day of his marriage, the death of his mother, the birth of each child and grandchild, the loss of a relative or a good friend.

He would take his children and later his grandchildren to share with them, his and their histories.

From time to time, there would be a reflection that this tree, that had grown and grown, blocking out one apple tree after another, would be better cut down for the good of the orchard.

But, as the years passed it became more and more a sort of family member and often his children or his children's children would go and talk or just sit with it in silent union.

And yet, not one flower nor fruit did it offer.

****

He became old and weak, full of aches and pains.

Finally, he was too weak to walk, his old bones and muscles no longer capable to hold or to move him.

His life had been full and rich, he was ready to release his hold on his frail existence – but not quite yet.

One day, the young son of the owner of the orchard, passing amongst the apple trees remarked something very particular.

The fruit was enormous, not surprisingly seeing the size the tree had grown to.

"Grandpa, grandpa, look, look, the tree has given a fruit for you".

They broke open the hardy, husk and fed him the succulent flesh with a baby's rubber spoon.

His old appetite returned; he ate it all.

"Get me my stick and coat and shoes".

The news travelled fast and wide and it was a parade of over twenty friends and family that accompanied the old master to visit his oldest living friend.

"Hello", he smiled, happily, "I've came to say goodbye".

He took a red ribbon and a black ribbon from his pocket and slowly tied them onto the same branch.

He gently kissed the soft, wrinkly bark with his own, soft, wrinkly lips.

They helped him sit, back propped against the solid, supporting wood. His legs, lost under the tangled, protruding roots.

Relaxing, he smiled, closed his eyes and leaned back into the tree.

Other Works

Island of Serenity Book 1
The Island of Survival

Pierre-Alain James 'Faron' Ferguson is about to commit suicide, in his suicide note he attempts to understand how he has come to have wrecked not only his own life, but also all of those around him.

Pierre-Alain James 'Faron' Ferguson finds himself in a type of 'no-mans-land', between here and there, he must accept to visit the 7 islands before he will be allowed to continue on to his next steps. The islands are named; Survival, Pleasure, Esteem, Love, Expression, Insight and lastly, the Island of Serenity

The Early Years:
Pierre-Alain James 'Faron' Ferguson is born into a well-to-do household of a factory owner, Scottish father and mother of a noble French family

He, and his younger brother Jay, grow up in a home of two distant but invested parents. Already, the first, small stones of his future problems are being put into place.

The Island of Survival:
Faron finds himself on the first of the seven islands, transformed into a prehistoric human form, he must learn how to interact with the local environment and the early humanoid tribe.

Here, he must reconnect with his instinct of survival.

Island of Serenity Book 2
Sun & Rain

This is the second chapter of Faron's life history, in which he falls in love, becomes a real cowboy, starts boarding school, finds his two best friends, goes to visit his weird aunt, goes skiing in Switzerland, and continues the relationship that brings him the greatest joy, yet the greatest sorrow in all of his life, but more than that would be telling too much.

FREE: If you have not yet read Book 1, Survival, no worries, I have included a shortened version, so as to introduce you to the story and the main characters.

Island of Serenity Book 3
The Island of Pleasure
Vol 1 Venice

Part 1.

Faron finds himself in a past version of Venice, as the owner
of an old but grand hotel that doubles as the meeting place
for the wealthy men of the City and the high-class escort girls
that live in the establishment.

Faron can do anything that he likes without limitation or cost.
Not only can he avail himself of the girls, but can eat and
drink, without limit, but never suffer from a hangover, nor
gain a gram.

So why has the enigmatic guide brought him here, and will
his limitless access to life's offerings really bring him the
pleasure that he is destined to experience?

Part 2.

 Faron is transformed into an adolescent tom boy. In this
more modern version of Venice, 'he' has just 7 days to be
made into a high-class escort girl.

What does this experience and the intrigues of the other
persons within his sphere, mean for him, on his continuing
quest to understand, and to experience, Pleasure?

Island of Serenity Book 4
The Island of Pleasure
Vol 2 Japan

Faron finds himself in the mystery of a long-ago Japan, in the body of a young, trainee Geisha.

Who is this sad, young man that he must help to find back his pleasure in life?

Why must he hide the identity of his mother, from the rest of the world?

Why was the love of his mother's life, stolen away by her sister, known to all as Madame Butterfly?

What part does the feudal lord of the region have in all this?

And how does Faron finally succeed to find the key to rediscovering pleasure in his life?

Island of Serenity Book 5
Rise and Fall

In this the 5th book of the series, we watch as Faron grows
from an adolescent into a young, driven man.

He begins by escaping to New York, before starting his
University career, finding back his two school, best friends,
Duncan and Mike.

After graduating, the three find themselves setting up a
business, manufacturing, buying and importing goods from
Indonesia.

Success seems to be just around the corner, but Faron cannot
help himself. Bitterness and betrayal, hound him like a
hungry dog.

To destroy, his own best friend, is not an act to
take lightly, but take it, he does.

And what of Angelique, and his daughter Aideen? He is still
emotionally entangled, but is that a good thing, or a very bad
thing?

Only time will tell.

Island of Serenity Book 6
The Island of Esteem pt1

The Knight's Tale

Faron, our anti-hero, finds himself transported into the body of Sir Lancelot, at the court of King Arthur.

He is on the quest to heal his self-esteem, but the knight, although noble and brave, is also a flawed human-being.

One person that avoids emotional conflicts but cannot escape his passion for Guinevere.

The knight has lost his memory, so he cannot remember how or why he has come to this point in his history.

And who is Al, his faithful squire who has helped him steal a magical sceptre from his supposed best friend, King Galahaut?

Follow Lancelot through his tortured romantic journey, in a world of court intrigue, magic and heroism.

Island of Serenity Book 7
The Island of Esteem pt2

'Le Morte D'Arthur

In this second and concluding volume of the Island of Esteem, we follow Al, as he continues to demonstrate to Faron, just what it means to be a hero.

Lancelot still is troubled by his past and present inability to impose himself, in any situation other than battle.

We get to understand how it was that Lancelot was forgiven by Guinevere, and why Arthur accepted to call on his help to retrieve the Uffington sceptre.

And how and why Al, chose and succeeded to steal it.

Also, how and why, he will be motivated to steal it, not just and second, but also a third time.

We follow the magical manipulations of Merlin and Morgan le Fey.

And finally, what happens to Lancelot and Al, before, during and after the final battle between Arthur and Mordred.

Adventures with the Master

Dhargey was a sickly child, or so his parents treated him.

He was too weak to join the army or work in the fields or even join the monastery as a normal trainee monk.

To explain to the 'Young Master' why he should be accepted into the order with a lightened program, he was forced to accompany the revered old man a little ways up the mountain.

As his parents watched him leave; somewhere they felt that they would never see their sickly, fragile boy ever again, somewhere they were totally right.

He was a happy, healthy seven year old until he witnessed the riders, dressed in red and black, destroying his village and murdering his parents; the trauma cut deep into his psyche.

Only the chance meeting with a wandering monk could set him back onto the road towards health and serenity.

Through meditation, initiations, stories, taming wild horses, becoming a monkey, mastering the staff and the sword; the future 'Young Master' prepares to face his greatest demon.

Two men, two journeys; one goal…

REMEMBER

Stories and poems for self-help and self-development based on techniques of Ericksonian and auto-hypnosis

Dusk falls, the world shrinks little by little into a smaller and smaller circle as the light continues to diminish.
The centre of this world is illuminated by a small, crackling sun; the flames dance, and the rough faces of the people gathered there are lit by the fire of their expectations.

The old man will begin to speak, he will explain to them how the world is, how it was, how it was created. He will help them understand how things have a sense, an order, a way that they need to be.
He will clarify the sources of un-wellness and unhappiness, what is sickness, where it comes from, how to notice it and… how to heal it.
To heal the sick, he will call forth the forces of the invisible realms, maybe he will sing, certainly he will talk, and talk, and talk.

Since the beginning of time we have gathered round those who can bring us the answers to our questions and the means to alleviate our sufferings.
This practice has not fundamentally changed since the earliest times; in every era, continent and culture we have found and continue to find these experiences.

In this, amongst the oldest of the healing traditions, he has succeeded to meld modern therapy theories and techniques with stories and poems of the highest quality.

With much humanity, clinical vignettes, common sense and lots of humour, the reader is gently carried from situation to situation.
Whether the problems described concern you directly, indirectly or not at all, you will surely find interest and benefits from the wealth of insights and advices contained within and the conscious or unconscious positive changes through reading the stories and poems.

None Fiction:

The Zen Approach to Modern Living Vol 1

Fundamentals, Family & Friends

Life is often experienced as a series of conflicts and aggressions, both from the outside and within ourselves.

The Zen Approach to Modern Living series, will lead you towards a more harmonious way of dealing with the many, complex and competing elements of your daily life.

These conflicts leave us exhausted, depressed, angry, and feeling generally unhappy and unfulfilled.

Being more in harmony with yourself will bring more happiness, more energy and open up the route to self-fulfilment.

Volume 1 covers; an introduction to the basic concepts, our relationship with ourselves, our family, (partner, children, parents, brothers, sisters and in-laws), friends and enemies.

Plus, plus, plus, A Bonus Chapter: My Deepest, Darkest, Secret.

The Zen approach to Low Impact Training and Sports

A simple method for achieving a healthy body and a healthy mind

Many of us approach our fitness and sports activities in an aggressive and competitive fashion.

And even if we feel that we succeed to break out of our comfort zones and win against ourselves or our opponent, there is an important cost to bear.

This level of violence that we have come to accept, so as to reach our goals is also an aggression against ourselves. By removing this need to 'win at any price', and tuning in with our bodies and emotions, we can achieve an enormous amount, all the while being in harmony with our mind, body and spirit.

The Zen approach to Low Impact Training and Sports, is a new softer approach where you can have the best of all worlds.

REMEMBER
Stories and poems for self-help and self-development based on
techniques of Ericksonian and auto-hypnosis

*Dusk falls, the world shrinks little by little into a smaller and smaller circle
as the light continues to diminish.*
*The centre of this world is illuminated by a small, crackling sun; the flames
dance, and the rough faces of the people gathered there are lit by the fire of
their expectations.*
*The old man will begin to speak, he will explain to them how the world is,
how it was, how it was created. He will help them understand how things
have a sense, an order, a way that they need to be.*
*He will clarify the sources of un-wellness and unhappiness, what is sickness,
where it comes from, how to notice it and... how to heal it.*
*To heal the sick, he will call forth the forces of the invisible realms, maybe
he will sing, certainly he will talk, and talk, and talk.*

Since the beginning of time we have gathered round those who can bring us
the answers to our questions and the means to alleviate our sufferings.
This practice has not fundamentally changed since the earliest times; in every
era, continent and culture we have found and continue to find these
experiences.

In this, amongst the oldest of the healing traditions, he has succeeded to meld
modern therapy theories and techniques with stories and poems of the highest
quality.

With much humanity, clinical vignettes, common sense and lots of humour,
the reader is gently carried from situation to situation. Whether the problems
described concern you directly, indirectly or not at all, you will surely find
interest and benefits from the wealth of insights and advices contained within
and the conscious or unconscious positive changes through reading the stories
and poems.

Picturing the Mind

Vol 1

A simple model capable to explain the functioning and
dysfunctioning of the human psyche.

Introduction to the Field theory of Human Functioning

For the average man and woman in the street, the complex and
competing theories and models of the human psyche; its
development, functioning and dis-functioning are often
unhelpful for their understanding of themselves.

This becomes even more problematic when they find
themselves in difficulty, as often, even the mental health
professionals, who are experts in their own fields, find
themselves at a loss to communicate successfully how and
why the patent is unwell and what needs to happen to find or
regain a healthy balance.

This opens up the question; 'is it possible to image a simple,
single model, accessible to everyone, to explain the
development, functioning and dis-functioning of the human
psyche?'

One that builds on existing theories and models, benefitting
from the mass of experience and research of 'modern western'
psychological concepts and ideas, but also integrating
traditional visions of the human psyche and modern theories
from the physical sciences.

Picturing the Mind, is an attempt to answer to this need.

Picturing the Mind
Vol 2

The second volume following on from the initial concepts will reflect on such subjects as:
  Relationships
  Exchanging energy
  Heart & Soul
  Recuperation
  Subjective constructions
  An unconscious yes, an unconscious no
  Me, myself and everyone else
  Circles in circles, the micro level
  Circles in circles, the macro level
  Intuition
  Metaphysical reflections

Picturing the Mind

Vol 3

Will deal with:

Psychopathology

Traditional psychotherapy
&
Alternative therapeutic approaches.